# EDGAR CAYCE'S GIFT

## Life-Changing Encounters with the Sleeping Prophet

CHRISTMAS 2024

To CAROLYN —

May these stories

reinspire you as they

did me!

With love — always,

Tom J. Todem

Selected Books by Kevin J. Todeschi

*The BEST Dream Book Ever*
*Divine Encounters: Experiences with God in Real Life*
*Dream Images and Symbols*
*Edgar Cayce on the Akashic Records*
*Edgar Cayce on Mastering Your Spiritual Growth*
*Edgar Cayce on Reincarnation and Family Karma*
*Edgar Cayce on Soul Mates and Soul Companions*
*Edgar Cayce on Vibrations*
*Edgar Cayce's Twelve Lessons in Personal Spirituality*

For additional titles, visit KevinTodeschi.com.

# EDGAR CAYCE'S GIFT

## Life-Changing Encounters with the Sleeping Prophet

### Kevin J. Todeschi

Yazdan Publishing

*Edgar Cayce's Gift:*
*Life-Changing Encounters with the Sleeping Prophet*

Copyright © 2024
by Kevin J. Todeschi

Yazdan Publishing Edition, October 2024

Printed in the United States of America

ISBN-13: 978-1-938838-21-7

Yazdan Publishing
P. O. Box 56545
Virginia Beach, VA  23456

Cover photo used by permission
of the Edgar Cayce Foundation, Virginia Beach, VA.

*To these individuals whose decades of commitment to the Edgar Cayce work brought transformational insights to countless thousands around the world.*

# Table of Contents

## *Foreword*
## Who Was Edgar Cayce?

Edgar Cayce (1877-1945) has been called "the Sleeping Prophet," "the father of Holistic medicine," "the miracle man of Virginia Beach," and "the most documented psychic of all time." For forty-three years of his adult life, he had the ability to put himself into some kind of self-induced sleep state by lying down on a couch, closing his eyes, and folding his hands over his stomach. This state of relaxation and meditation enabled him to place his mind in contact with all time and space and gave him the ability to respond to any question he was asked. His responses came to be called "readings" and contain insights so valuable that even to this day Edgar Cayce's work is known and studied throughout the world. Hundreds of books have explored his amazing psychic gift, and the entire range of Cayce material is accessed by tens of thousands of people daily via the Internet.

Although the vast majority of the Cayce material deals with health and every manner of illness, countless topics were explored by Cayce's psychic talent and include dreams, philosophy, intuition, business advice, the Bible, education, childrearing, ancient civilizations, personal spirituality, improving human relationships, and much more. In fact, during Cayce's lifetime, he discussed thousands of different subjects, and the Edgar Cayce database of readings consists of a mind-boggling 24 million words!

The Cayce legacy presents a body of information so valuable that Edgar Cayce himself might have hesitated to predict their impact on contemporary society. Who could have known that terms such as meditation, auras, spiritual growth, reincarnation, psychic ability, dreams, and holism would become household words to millions? For decades, the Cayce readings have stood the test of time, research, and extensive study. Further details of Cayce's life and work are explored in such classic books as *There Is a River* by Thomas Sugrue, *Many Mansions* by Gina Cerminara, and *Edgar Cayce: An American Prophet* by Sidney Kirkpatrick. A wealth of information and programs can also be found at EdgarCayce.org.

Edgar Cayce was born and raised on a farm near Hopkinsville, Kentucky. He had a normal childhood in many respects. However, he could see the glowing energy patterns that surround individuals. At a very early age, he told his parents that he could see and talk with his grandfather—who was deceased. Later, he developed the ability to sleep on his schoolbooks and retain a photographic memory of their entire contents.

As the years passed, he met and fell in love with Gertrude Evans, who would become his wife. Shortly thereafter, he developed a paralysis of the vocal cords and could scarcely speak above a whisper. Everything was tried, but no physician was able to locate a cause. The laryngitis persisted for months. As a last resort, hypnosis was tried. Cayce put himself to sleep and was asked by a specialist to describe the problem. While asleep he spoke normally, diagnosing the ailment and prescribing a simple treatment. After the recommendations were followed, Edgar Cayce could speak normally for the first time in almost a year! The date was March 31, 1901 — that was the first reading.

When it was discovered what had happened, many others began to want help. It was soon learned that Edgar Cayce could put himself into this unconscious state and give readings for anyone — regardless of where they were. If the advice was followed, they got well. Newspapers throughout the country carried articles about his work, but it wasn't until Gertrude was stricken with tuberculosis that the readings were brought home to him. Even with medical treatments, she continued to grow worse and was not expected to live. Finally, the doctors said there was nothing more they could do. A reading was given and recommended such things as osteopathy, hydrotherapy, inhalants, dietary changes, and prescription medication. The advice was followed and Gertrude returned to perfectly normal health. Over time, countless others found that they too were healed, helped, and personally transformed by information given to them in Cayce readings.

This volume consists of interviews and personal memories by those who knew him best — Edgar Cayce's contemporaries. Some of these individuals detail how they first came in contact with Edgar Cayce. Others discuss their own experiences with the readings and the Cayce work. For decades, each of these people inspired countless audiences with personal stories of their experiences with Cayce and the readings. Without exception, each of them was convinced that their interactions with Edgar Cayce and his work had a tremendous impact on their life's direction, changing them forever. As amazing as some of their experiences sound, they are not unusual. Even to this day, the Cayce work continues to profoundly change peoples' lives — physically, mentally, and spiritually.

Throughout his life, Edgar Cayce claimed no special abilities nor did he ever consider himself to be some kind of twentieth-century prophet. The readings never offered a set of beliefs that had to be embraced, but instead focused on the fact that each person should test in his or her own life the principles presented. Although Cayce himself was a Christian and read the Bible from cover to cover every year of his life, his work was one that stressed the importance of comparative study among belief systems all over the world. The underlying principle of the readings is the oneness of all life, love for all people, and compassion and understanding for every major religion in the world.

Having been involved with the Cayce work for fifty years, I had the wonderful opportunity to know, hear, and interact with many of these individuals whose memories of Cayce became instrumental in transforming my own life. These were real people, who had very real experiences with one of the most incredible men of the twentieth century. Their personal encounters with Edgar Cayce changed their lives, and their memories of that experience continued to touch, inspire, and transform others, even for decades after Cayce had passed away.

Their stories are presented here with the hope that it will continue to help people change their lives for the better.

Kevin J. Todeschi

## *Chapter One*
# HUGH LYNN CAYCE

*Perhaps more than anyone, Hugh Lynn Cayce (1907-1982) was responsible for taking A.R.E. – the organization founded by his father, Edgar Cayce, in 1931 – from its humble beginnings and turning it into one of international renown.*

*Instrumental in developing widespread recognition and acceptance of subjects, such as psychical research, dream analysis, meditation, and personal spiritual development, Hugh Lynn received critical praise for his first book* Venture Inward. *He was awarded the title of first citizen of Virginia Beach in 1964. He was known for his commitment and enthusiasm for working with young people. He was a dynamic and popular speaker.*

*This is a compilation of some of Hugh Lynn's talks over the years, including material from what would be his last address to the A.R.E. Congress during its 50th anniversary.*

My father was born on a farm outside of Hopkinsville, Kentucky, in 1877. When he was a schoolboy, he was having problems remembering anything he had studied, and one night – while working with his father who was trying to push him through a spelling lesson – he asked his father to let him go to sleep for a while. He fell asleep for about ten minutes on the book he had been struggling with, and when he woke up, he knew everything in that book! From that point on, he could sleep on a book and memorize its contents. He became known as the sleeping Cayce. He didn't have a formal education; he eventually left school.

When he was a young man, he developed laryngitis. Doctors tried to work with him, trying to cure this but they couldn't do anything to help him. It persisted for almost a year. Finally, they resorted to hypnosis because they could find nothing physically wrong with him, and he was somehow able to speak in the unconscious state. They let him put himself to sleep and asked him to describe his physical condition and what could be done about it. He did just that, and he got well.

A group of doctors from Hopkinsville and Bowling Green, Kentucky, began to study him, and in 1910, Dr. Wesley Ketchum wrote a paper about him for a clinical research society in Boston. This was published in *The New York Times*—headlines were picked up in papers all across the country about a farmer boy who became a doctor when hypnotized. People began to ask for his help from all over. In time, the readings covered every topic imaginable.

When I was between six and seven years old and my father was working as a photographer, I got ahold of a large box of flashlight powder that my father used. In those days you had to flash this powder with a cap and hold it up above your head and then click the camera at the same time. I put a little bit of this powder on the floor and was going to scare a maid with this when she came into the dark room. Well, the match head must have gone into the box, because the whole box of flashlight powder exploded in my face. For weeks, I was blind.

The flash burns were so severe that the doctors felt that the eyes could not be saved without taking one of them out. Our family physician told me this, and it was then that I asked my father to give a reading. When the treatments he recommended were applied, in applications on the eyes, internal medicine, and a change of diet, the eyes began to heal. When they took the bandages off of my eyes about three months later, and I could see, I began to think of Edgar Cayce quite differently—not only as a father but as someone who had saved my eyesight.

In the early 1930s, I was with him in New York when he was giving a psychic reading on someone who was in the room, and there were about forty or fifty people present. He was lying on a studio couch in the center of the room with people sitting all around him. In the middle of the reading, he was talking. A man wrote a question on a piece of paper, got up, and passed it to me across Edgar Cayce's body. Now, the moment the paper went over his body, he stopped talking, and for the next twenty or thirty minutes, I was trying to get him to go on; and then for another twenty or thirty minutes, I was trying to get him to wake up. He wouldn't do either. He had just stopped talking instantaneously.

Finally, I repeated the suggestion that the body would be normalized, and the circulation would be equalized, and that he would wake up feeling good, relaxed, and so forth. He began to react in a very strange way in front of all of these people. With his hands crossed over his solar plex, and lying on the studio couch, he suddenly came to a standing position at the end of the couch, as if someone had put their hands on the back of his head and set him up straight. He was dizzy. He was awake, and he had to get out of the room very quickly. He was upset. He had a glass of milk and a cracker, and when he came back he felt fine. He was all right.

We then asked questions. What went on? What

happened? It was then that he told us for the first time that there was a finer physical body, lying parallel to the flesh body. Apparently, he went out of his body every time he gave readings. We asked a lot of questions. His answers would lead us to believe that this is a body that is moving at a much faster vibratory rate — it interpenetrates the flesh body constantly. In sleep, it frequently moves out, and we have what are called "out-of-body experiences." He would indicate also that it is this body that we use at the moment of death — a finer body moving at a faster vibratory rate.

During Edgar Cayce's lifetime, and particularly during the closing years of his life, he was able to see energy patterns around people, and could at a conscious level read these in terms of color . . . I watched him go around a group of thirty or forty people and pick up physical, emotional, and mental patterns, as he described the color of the aura around each of them.

My father was an unusually creative person. He was a fine photographer and was noted for his pictures, especially those of children. He was an inventor of games. He loved to play all kinds of games and invented one called Pit, which is still on the market. He was a fine bowler; I never won a bowling game with him. He was a lousy golfer, but he loved to play. He was a great fisherman and fished everywhere that he had an opportunity. He was a man who loved to cook and did all kinds of things with preserves and berries of various kinds. He was a great gardener and loved to have exotic trees of all kinds around him. He was a man who was a fine Sunday School teacher — the best, I think, I ever knew — and always had the largest classes in any church that he worked in. He also had Sunday School classes in prisons, wherever he happened to be. This was quite a remarkably creative man, though he never had any formal education.

The work that he did has been placed in Virginia Beach, Virginia, in the form of written records, letters, and reports. And with the readings and their reports, these readings have become the basis for a gradual and steady program of research—documentary and experimental. These readings have touched the lives of thousands of people. They are like pieces in a vast puzzle, which, when put together, begin to show the pattern of certain law and order. Patterns that, when studied, understood, and obeyed can bring to individuals some sense of balance, some sense of how to meet problems.

It would be very foolish for us to simply build on the revelations of Edgar Cayce—he would be the last person to have called them such. Instead, we should take the readings and take what we find to be good—test it, work with it, and then build a point of view for ourselves upon the results.

When talking about Edgar Cayce, I have used a simile of with which I'm sure every single one of you is familiar. Have you ever looked into a telescope out into the starry heavens at night and seen stars that you hadn't seen before—catching a glimpse of the tremendous scope and range of the universe floating away in eternity? I'm sure some of you have caught that. Perhaps in high school or college, you've turned to a microscope, slid a drop of clear water under the microscope lens, looked through it, and suddenly saw a drop of water come alive with all kinds of movement, and you realize, again, the tremendous range of God's creation—a range beyond your sense perception. Living with a man like Edgar Cayce and watching him day by day give readings to people who came with all kinds of problems was like looking through a telescope or a microscope. It opened up a new perception, a new range of understanding, far beyond anything that one could link with the five senses.

There is, of course, the health material. I think the preventative material in the Edgar Cayce readings is so exciting in terms of diet, exercise, massage, and the sweats and the packs and the baths, and all the things that go into it. For example, do any of you have tendencies toward arthritis? You have a terrific opportunity to look at the readings and become familiar with whole patterns of diet that will stop you from hurting now, and keep you from hurting for a long time. And then, if you slap a little peanut oil on you in the right places, it will keep you greased and oiled so that you wiggle right along in much better condition. And it won't be so painful! Now that's preventative. I'm using that only as an illustration for there are diet patterns in the readings for every tendency.

Edgar Cayce was famous for many, many years as a medical clairvoyant. Then in 1923, he began to give two new kinds of readings: readings on dreams, and the famous life readings that spoke of reincarnation and karma—ideas which were strange to him at the time. Gina Cerminara, a psychologist, was the first to examine this concept so beautifully in *Many Mansions* — the concept of the survival of the real essence of the self through many reincarnation experiences on the earth plane. It is examined in a practical way, focusing on the everyday problems of individuals, relating it to the depth of an individual's talents, wisdom, and abilities, describing it, and relating it to the individual case so that you and I perhaps may come to a better understanding of how to really see the total picture of the self.

For me, karma is simply memory. Nothing else. You and I have no karma with each other. There's nothing between people. There is only memory in relationship to each other, which is quite different because it's a memory buried in me or it's buried in you, what you remember is what you have to deal with in terms of your own karma.

This is what Jesus was talking about when he spoke about thought patterns and thoughts. He didn't call it patterns, but he said you don't have to commit something for it to affect you. All you have to do is *think* about it. And he was very specific. He was talking to some men and he said, if you just lust after a woman, you have already committed the act. And you pay for that. Don't kid yourself. You don't have to do it. You don't have to fulfill it at a body level. All you have to do is think about it. So the beginning here is in the mind, the patterns are built there, and we store them.

You've got a beautiful setup in the readings if you want to begin to deal with your karma as memory. Look around you. Pick out the best relationships of your life and deepen them, enrich them. But also, pick out the worst ones, the difficult ones. Deal with those, don't leave them hanging, don't let them go; don't pass them by, because they grow. Things repeat themselves with karmic memories and create strong, deep emotions.

Edgar Cayce talked about how our lives in the earth brought these tremendous emotional urgings that we possess. This is one of the reasons, I think, these urges come through the endocrines, because of the strong emotional relationship. We have the opportunity to deal with the worst and the best. Sometimes you just can't avoid it; I couldn't. I arrived in the earth and by golly here were a couple of my memories holding me — my Poppa and my Momma. And I had a time. I had a rough time with Edgar Cayce. For me, he was far more than just a father, a very good one, far more than just a good Sunday School teacher, far more than the greatest psychic I've ever seen come down the tracks. And I've looked at a lot of them. He was many other things, too, that I had to face and deal with. And yet, fortunately, he was also the most loving person I have ever known. And it was beautiful to deal with my jealousy and my hate, for it was that at the time, in the light of his love that he was able to transmit. It was a beautiful experience, and it worked out. I've cleaned up a lot of stuff.

Dad didn't hold onto things like I did. I'd been holding onto things for 10,000 years! He turned them loose. He could get mad at me quicker than he could at anybody else, but he would get over it. It would pass. He didn't hold these things in the thought patterns, and we have a tendency to hold onto them and keep reactivating them.

I have used this crazy illustration before. I was in a cab with a man in New York once. He had a violent argument with the cab driver over the fare. They almost had a fight. Afterwards, we went upstairs to meet with a lot of people. There was a big group standing around and this man was reliving what he had said to the taxicab driver all over again. And he was red in the face, and he was saying a lot of things he hadn't said that he wished he had said. Craziest thing!

We can catch ourselves if we watch ourselves. Dad didn't hold onto this kind of thing. He would blow up, but turn loose of it very quickly. You don't feed these things, these negative karmic patterns, or they grow. And they get so big, they really swamp you. The stuff that spills out of the unconscious, you can't handle. It blasts you, and you slip. What breaks, of course, is the body, the flesh. And you begin to suffer. And then you wonder what in the world is wrong with me? And you have set the pattern for this. You've torn yourself apart. You've made yourself sick emotionally, and mentally, and then it reproduces itself in the flesh. All of psychosomatic medicine, of course, is telling us this.

A better approach to our challenges with one another is confessional prayer. I'm a great believer in confessional prayer. Now there are some things you can go out and talk to your best friend about. Some things you can sit down and share with your wife or your husband or son or a daughter, mother or father — somebody related. But there are other things that you need to work with that you just deal with in your mind with God. And this is confessional prayer — that business of forgiving yourself, and then asking God's forgiveness. Now do this while you're looking at the face of the person you are having the difficulty with. And you hold this. And you can do this every day until it goes away. It won't take you but about a week to get rid of something you've been carrying around this life. And fourteen days will clean up several thousand years!

You forgive yourself for what you've done and said to this face that you're looking at. And then you ask God's forgiveness. Then you forgive the face, the person, and then you bless, and put light around that individual, and you love that face. You do this regularly for a while and the relationship will clear and clean up. You know what happens? It's wonderful! The other person seems to get a lot better. Of course, we begin to change, too, within ourselves. We need to work diligently and persistently. There's a phrase for it in the readings. It's line upon line, here a little, there a little, precept upon, precept. But continuously working at it and gradually getting rid of it. So often the readings refer to the dynamic of "Mind is the builder." The Edgar Cayce readings suggest that the mind is actually something that exists in every cell of the body, and it is building, building constantly.

I frequently answer the telephone, and often it's a person who is in trouble—all kinds of trouble. Now, whether I am on the phone or sitting talking, I start praying, instantaneously, because I want to connect. I begin to try to work with energy and light around the individual and whatever they're talking about, whatever they're doing, whatever the voice is saying over the phone while I listen. And this helps me focus. It helps me listen. I think in a way, when you begin to pray for and deal with a spiritual energy in a person and that's what you look for, prayer stimulates spiritual life in other people. It is not just protective for you in any sense. It's a connection, and it's worked for me.

Let me talk for a moment about the nature of the soul, and it's purpose here. The application of spiritual law—applying it on a daily level, and the lifting of consciousness through what the readings have described again and again as meditation—is the very thing that can put you in touch with your soul self. If you asked me to give you a group of the Edgar Cayce psychic readings which would be of the greatest help to you, I would not hesitate one moment in handing you the 130 readings that were given as the basis for the two books, A Search for God, books one and two. Second, I would tell you without question that without the study group inspiration, without the continued group prayer, it would have been impossible for me to have ever achieved what has happened with the A.R.E. since its early days.

It was the beginning of the study group program in which Dad suggested a new and dynamic approach to—not only study but to experiment with and test in daily life—the spiritual concepts that flowed through this altered state of consciousness that he worked from for more than forty-three years. You can become a channel through which this creative power and energy begins to flow to those you touch—your family, your children, your husband, your wife, your mother, your father, your neighbors, your friends, and your business associates. It is going to begin to change you, and as it changes you, it is going to begin to change the attitudes of other people with whom you associate day by day. The result is going to be the healing of your environment, your city, and the nation—perhaps a contribution to the world, for we are beginning to be a part of the consciousness of the whole.

In all our relations with one another, we are either building or destroying. I'm absolutely certain of it. I don't think there is any middle ground. Sometimes it's rough, and many of you who are in study groups know that the suggestion that you just take whoever shows up and deal with it is not always easy. People show up that you would not be caught with anywhere else. I think that all of you are going to have to come to the realization that as you begin to pray for people, as you begin to try to reach out and share what you have found to be good, more people are going to show up on your doorstep. More people are going to be in touch with you, and they are going to be in trouble. They have needs, and you are not going to be prepared to handle all of those needs, and you shouldn't try in many instances to handle them all. But you should be prepared to know how to be discerning enough to recognize who you can work with, and who should be sent to specialists.

You will fail and get discouraged. I have failed many, many, many times. I have failed more times on most of these procedures than there are people here in this room. It's easy to fail when you're working like this. But the successes are so rich and so wonderful. They're so worthwhile. And you begin to recognize that you can be used by God wherever you are and whoever you are. You can do things far beyond your capacity because you are dealing, not with your energy—for none of us has any energy—but with God's. Now there is something positive in every human being. Sometimes you have to look very hard to find it, but most of us don't see very well. It's not that it's not there. We just can't see it.

Many years ago now, I had a heart attack—a very small heart attack. I had it right here in this room. It started here and continued long enough for them to get it on an electroencephalograph so they knew what it looked like. It turned out to be mild, but it put me in the hospital for a little while. They were very careful and cautious about heart attacks, and I stayed there for a while, and got all involved in the hospital activities.

After I came home, I realized that there were a lot of things in my life I needed to change—including my meditation and prayer time and my Bible reading and inspirational reading. So I doubled what I had been doing, and then I doubled that. I think you'll find this to be true: when you push yourself in quietness and prayer, dreams become very interesting. I had an interesting dream.

Morton and Edmund Blumenthal and my father and my mother—a lot of people that had been with the early organization—were there. And Morton was telling me, "Hugh Lynn, everything's been straightened out over here. It's all right now. The A.R.E. is going to have energy that it never had before." He said, and he used his simile, "It's like money in the bank. You could write a check on it for any amount!"

And Dad said, "Yeah, Hugh Lynn, anything you can dream of can come about now."

If you knew those people, if you had known them — you'd know what I mean — just the idea of that happening on that level, the possibility that this took place, is a healing that can extend over to every one of our lives in a very rich and wonderful fashion.

The Edgar Cayce material has this focus and emphasis on the spiritual nature of us and the tremendous capacity that we all have to reach far beyond ourselves. Edgar Cayce came, I think, to help prepare a way for this consciousness to develop. And I wanted to help, of course. But the thing that strikes you almost immediately, and I even mentioned it fifty years ago, is that Edgar Cayce was saying and challenging from the very beginning of the first readings that this was not unique, was not a phenomenon, was not different. It was simply possible for us all. We all have this quality, and it's a quality of a spiritual nature. It's the soul, and it's within us all.

I have found in the A.R.E. the finest vehicle for serving and for loving that I know about, and that's what He said to do. Sooner or later you'll all come to deal with this and face this. Perhaps not in the exact terms of that name, which represents a long mystical experience of God's expression on Earth — the Christ Consciousness — but this is the name I use. A.R.E. has been a vehicle, a structure, and a way to work with those principles. How can you love people — that's what He said do — how can you serve people? How can you go about achieving and doing this, unless you begin to share the best that you know with each individual you meet, without exception?

I have found in the readings of Edgar Cayce, and I found them in the life of the man that I knew as Edgar Cayce, a way to achieve and focus for thousands of people a very practical approach to this business of love and service.

## Chapter Two
# GLADYS DAVIS TURNER

*Gladys Davis Turner (1905-1986) served as Edgar Cayce's secretary from 1923 until his death in 1945. In addition to serving on the Boards of A.R.E., the Edgar Cayce Foundation, and Atlantic University as corporate secretary, she was considered the central guardian of the Cayce legacy, as well as staff historian. Many individuals credit Gladys with preserving the readings after Mr. Cayce's death.*

*Gladys supervised an 11-year project cataloging and indexing the Cayce readings, making them available to an ever-broadening audience. Over the years, Gladys's skills as a historian and her memory of readings, personalities, and events proved invaluable for the organization, researchers, and members throughout the world. One of her final projects before her death was to oversee the fundraising effort to computerize the Edgar Cayce readings.*

*This information is taken from interviews with Gladys in 1975 and 1984.*

I met Edgar Cayce about a year before I went to work for him. My sister was in Hugh Lynn Cayce's class in grade school, and they were good friends. I met Hugh Lynn before I met Mr. Cayce. Hugh Lynn would come home with my sister, swinging her books.

My sister had started Sunday School at the First Christian Church where the Cayces attended, and she, Hugh Lynn, and a lot of other young people were in Mr. Cayce's Christian Endeavour group. They went to a convention of the Christian Endeavour Society in Birmingham. Mr. and Mrs. Cayce took this group, and my sister was among them. I walked her to the train, which was about three blocks from our house, with my father, and met Mr. and Mrs. Cayce then. A girlfriend of mine had mentioned Mr. Cayce giving readings, but at the time I thought she was talking about Edgar Cayce's father, who they called Mr. "L.B." I didn't realize it was Edgar Cayce giving the readings until 1923, a year later.

I was working as a stenographer at Tissier Hardware Company, a wholesale and retail store in the area that had everything in it. You could buy all kinds of things there. You could buy your lunch if you wanted to; it also had a dry goods department. I was in an office in the middle of this building, and I did the stenographic work for about three men. I was in the office of the Office Manager, who was the accountant for the organization. They sold plows and all kinds of farm machinery and had salesmen going out.

A lady by the name of Miss Willie Graham was in charge of the chinaware department. She asked the office if I could come with her about two or three times to a hotel where a salesman would be displaying chinaware. She'd have me take down the story of the chinaware pattern — type it up so she could make copies to give to her customers.

In August 1923, Miss Graham asked me if I would go with her to take down a reading she was having for her sick nephew. He was in Birmingham with her brother and his wife. The Cayce studio was on the second floor, right off Broad Street. It was catty cornered across from

Tissier Hardware, so we just had to walk across the
street.

Mr. Cayce met us at the top of the steps and took us
to this little room, which was in back of his darkroom;
there were other people sitting there in the room. He
sat on a cot and talked to us a while, then he put his
hands at the back of his head and lay there for a few
minutes just looking at the ceiling. Next, he moved his
hands down across his solar plexus before starting with
the reading. He was in his shirtsleeves—the books all
say he loosened his collar and tie and all, but he didn't
have one on that day.

Cayce's father, Mr. L.B., was conducting the reading,
and he started to talk to him and give Edgar Cayce
the suggestion. I found out later that the suggestion
was given when Mr. Cayce's eyes began to flutter. He
started breathing, with his chest going up and down.
Mr. L.B. gave him the suggestion to help this boy and
the address where he was and Edgar Cayce said, "Yes,
we have the body" and started giving the reading. I was
so busy taking it down, I didn't really think of it as any
other job than taking dictation.

I found out later that some of the other people in the
room were there trying out for the job of stenographer.
Later, Mr. Cayce said that I made the best copy of
anybody taking a reading, and he offered me the job.
I felt good about that—but years later I thought, "Well,
my goodness, how did he know? He didn't even read
it!"

This was a Thursday afternoon. Miss Graham told
me that I was to type it out and make two copies of it.
Afterward, I read my notes to a friend and asked her to
help with the spelling of some of the words I had never
heard of things such as "dorsals" and "cervicals," and
so forth.

I went back to work Friday morning at the hardware store, typed off the reading, and made two copies. I must not have been very busy that morning. At lunchtime, Miss Graham took one copy to Mr. Cayce. And when she came back from lunch she came in and said, "Mr. Cayce told me to ask you to think about coming to work for him. If you are interested, come up and see him." And she added, "I think you should do it." I never had a doubt. I knew I wanted to do it. I was bored. You know, I think the year before that I was so restless. I wanted to do something but didn't know what, so I took the job.

I liked Mr. Cayce immediately. I felt comfortable with him. I think it was because I had never really had any adult, a man especially, talk to me like I was an equal really. Instead of talking down to me, he seemed actually interested in me as a person. I found out he was that way with everybody. So it wasn't anything unusual for him. I went back to the hardware store and gave two-weeks-notice, and it was two weeks later I went to work for him on September 10, 1923.

One of the first things Mr. Cayce said to me was, "Remember, Miss Gladys" — I think it was the first day I went to work — "Remember, Miss Gladys, you'll be working with me, not for me." That was the way it was.

I felt an instant attraction to this man. I just trusted him. I didn't think anything about his readings, when I sat there and listened to it, it was just like any other job of taking dictation. One day, during a reading, he said a string of words. So I was wondering whether I should put a dash or a comma — just how to word this — and over there, asleep, on the couch, his eyes closed, he said, "Put a comma between these." Other people learned that it was good to be present for the reading because if they thought of questions, he would answer them without being asked.

One of the early readings that was so startling to me happened when we were in New York in 1925. This lady was having a reading for her son, who was ill, and at the end of this reading, after Mrs. Cayce had given him the suggestion to wake up, he started talking again. He said, "We have here the body of Clara Enlow; we would advise that she have surgery for this condition . . ."

I didn't know who Clara Enlow was, where she lived, or anything. We got back to Dayton two or three days later and there was a letter from this lady saying that the doctors had advised her to have this surgery and she just wanted his advice first before she did it. She was apparently just thinking about him, and getting his advice, and the reading came through.

Early on, I just accepted what I was doing even though some of the things I didn't understand. I had never seen anything like it, but a lot of things I hadn't seen before. Through the years, however, we were all inspired by the readings — all of us close in the family there. And we'd listen to a reading and it would just give us courage and new hope and everything. But Mr. Cayce didn't have that, he didn't hear the readings; he would only know what we told him. He'd ask, "Did you get a good reading?" or whatever, and then if something exciting was in it, we'd tell him about it.

We were constantly encouraged. We'd get a reading on the Work and it would encourage us. The study group readings were just full of encouragement. They'd give you something for you to understand yourself, be a better person, and do what you were supposed to do in this incarnation. Mr. Cayce was encouraged by how people told him they had been helped. That made it all worthwhile. He believed that his work was God-given or he wouldn't have stayed with it.

The first real mention of reincarnation occurred in a reading given in Dayton, Ohio. I had been with Mr. Cayce less than a month when Arthur Lammers came to Selma. He was impressed with Mr. Cayce and took him back to Dayton. When he left, he asked Mrs. Cayce to read me the old readings. At the time, they had copies of only about 600 readings that were in a cardboard box, alphabetically by name. A lot of different people had taken them down. No copies were made of many of the early readings.

Mr. Cayce left with Mr. Lammers and Mrs. Cayce was asked to give me experience with the readings by reading these old copies to me and letting me take them down just to keep me busy, I guess. So I did that. And then after that, we'd talk. It was wonderful. She told me all about the family, her family and his, and how they had been sweethearts since they were in their teens. It was fascinating. I used to love to read love stories, you know, all through my teens, and I was scared to death of boys but I liked love stories.

While he was in Dayton, Mrs. Cayce would get a letter from Mr. Cayce and she would tell me what he said and everything. One day she came to me and said that Edgar wanted to move to Dayton. "Do you want to come with us?" I certainly did. There was no doubt in my mind. So we went to Dayton. And when we got there, they had already gotten readings. Arthur Lammers was interested in astrology and he asked Mr. Cayce if he would give him an astrology reading. It was in this reading that mentioned certain characteristics of Mr. Lammers and made a statement almost like a side remark, "He was once a monk."

After that, Mr. Lammers and some of the people with him wanted to have other readings dealing with reincarnation to find out who they had been. Edgar

Cayce had a reading with a group of others — Arthur
Lammers, Linden Shroyer, and George Klingensmith.
In the reading, it said that the four of them had been
associated during the Trojan Period for "destructive
purposes." Instead of gaining in soul development at
the time, they had lost. It recommended that this time
around they should work together to be constructive.

Although Mr. Cayce seemed to be fascinated, he
wasn't sure that it was right. He just questioned it. But
still, when we got there, he was telling us about this, and
he began getting readings for the members of his family.
He got one for Gertrude, one for little Edgar Evans who
was five years old and he got one for Hugh Lynn who
was in Selma. He had stayed in Selma to finish out the
school year. And Hugh Lynn — I've heard him on the
lecture platform tell about how horrified he was when
he came to Dayton and was given the life reading for his
Christmas present. Mr. Cayce offered to give me a life
reading too. It was very unusual for him to offer to give
anybody a reading, but I saw it happen several times,
you know, when he felt he'd like to see a reading on
somebody.

My life reading said some wonderful things that
certainly have come true. One of them was "One who
with others will draw many of the more beautiful things
of the earth plane about them." Well, that has happened.
It's happened, and all of you are a part of it — everybody
in the Work. It's just a wonderful thing. And when people
ask me about how I reacted, it was just all so new to me. I
was given the eighth life reading that he had given. The
only things that I knew for certain were true was he said
that I had a "distrust" of the opposite sex from a French
incarnation, and that I had a fear of knives and cutting
instruments from the Persian period, when I had been
wounded by the sword and lingered, suffering.

I knew those two things were true because I would never have a date with a boy by myself. I'd go with a girlfriend, have a double date, get her date to bring somebody, and that went on for quite a bit. That was very satisfactory. I didn't want to be alone with one. I have long since overcome my distrust of the opposite sex, but I still have a fear of knives.

I also had a number of physical readings. I was having trouble with headaches, and I was wearing glasses. I had had glasses for about two years. The doctor prescribed these glasses for eyestrain. I had been working under a skylight, you know, and they had a colored awning, and I'd sit there at my desk in the shadow of it, and I didn't think anything about it. The doctor said that's what had caused my eyes to hurt. He said to wear these glasses all the time.

So I was having headaches up there in Dayton, and Mr. Cayce offered to give me a reading. So right off in the reading, he said, "Take off the glasses. You don't need them." There was an intimation that I might someday have to have glasses, but it wasn't any time soon. The problem had been caused from poor circulation and from poor posture. He said, "Sit up straight!" You know, instead of leaning over your work; I've tried to pay attention to that through the years. The readings also suggested I use head and neck exercises to stimulate circulation, and the Violet Ray around the neck and down, between my shoulders and so on, which I did.

When I took my glasses off, the headaches stopped immediately. I didn't have to wear glasses until I was in my late 40s really. I was farsighted, and the reading mentioned that and mentioned the left eye being weaker than the right.

On another occasion, I had a physical reading after going to the dentist. I remember going to the dentist, and he said that he'd never seen anybody with worst tonsils than I had—just awful. He told me that I needed to have them taken out and the sooner the better. So I had a reading for that, and the reading said that the tonsils were there for a purpose, they should not be taken out unless absolutely necessary, and it might someday be necessary, but not now. They were needed in the body like a wastebasket, the poisons went through the tonsils to be eliminated. It wasn't until after we moved to Virginia Beach, about two or three years before Mr. Cayce died, that I was having trouble and Mr. Cayce said, "Time to take out the tonsils now. They've done their job, so take them out." I had them taken out right then, and never had any problem at all.

It was really Tom Sugrue's book, *There Is a River*, that had a positive impact on Mr. Cayce's work. His book brought a lot of people into the Work with an understanding of what it was all about. On the other hand, the article "Miracle Man of Virginia Beach," which appeared in *Coronet* magazine in September 1943, made people think that miracles were available and all you had to do was call up Virginia Beach and get an appointment with his secretary. It was just a deluge!

Mr. Cayce just couldn't cope with it. He had appointments two years in advance when he died. People were sending in their money, and we had to finally stop taking appointments when Mr. Cayce became ill in August of 1944. After he died, we returned all of the money we had received in advance, which was about $13,000.

He felt such a need to help people. I remember Mrs. Cayce pleading with him to stop working so much, and he'd say, "I've got to." Instead of giving two readings a day, he'd double up. Instead of giving one reading, devoting the whole time to one person, he'd give five

or six or more. One time, we had seven or eight, or
something like that. It was just awful.

Mr. Cayce would pore over the correspondence. He
was trying to do it all himself—all these bags of mail
just coming in. He would sit and pore over these letters
and feel sorry for the people. You know, they would
complain about the awful condition they were in, this,
that, and the other. Mrs. Cayce just begged him, she
said, "You've just got to stop this!" And he said, "I can't!
I've got to help these people, just got to." And she said,
"Well, Edgar, if you keep on like you're going, pretty
soon you won't be able to help anybody." He said, "I
know it, but I'll just keep on as long as I can and then I'll
be through." And that's what he did.

Hugh Lynn and Edgar Evans were both overseas.
If Hugh Lynn had been home, I think he could have
handled it because Mr. Cayce trusted him. Mr. Cayce
did not take care of himself. He would follow the
readings for himself for a little while, but he wasn't
consistent. One of the last things that he was told to do
was to get osteopathic treatments—three osteopathic
treatments a week, and to do these packs, and a lot of
things he was supposed to do to help himself. Well, it
was the war years and we didn't have the gas to come
and go. Besides, if he had gone into Norfolk—we had
no osteopath in Virginia Beach—three times a week, it
would take up at least a half a day, even if we could get
gas. He just couldn't do that. I mean he wouldn't be able
to give the readings, you see. So he decided he would
just try and keep up with the readings.

Everybody pleaded with him to rest. Dr. Henry
George was an osteopath from Wilmington, Delaware,
who had come to the A.R.E. Congress that year. He told
him that he just had to rest and he had to get away and
so they asked in a reading where to go, and the reading

suggested Roanoke. Mr. Cayce had been up there and liked it. They drove to Roanoke and stayed in a hotel. He got into the hands of a doctor there who we all felt went off on a tangent. Instead of following the readings, this doctor had his own system of treating him. We didn't know that he was not following the readings. The treatment was not a success, and he was brought home. Mr. Cayce died in January 1945. Mrs. Cayce passed away in April, a few months later.

I just felt like I belonged with Edgar Cayce and his family, and I never left them. All through the years, I became one of the family. As far as I'm concerned, the greatest thing he gave to me is the realization that we are responsible for our own destiny. He also explained the close relationship we all have with God, as well as the understanding I have of Jesus. He just made the Bible come alive for me personally. He gave me an understanding of life that I wouldn't have otherwise. He's done these same things for a lot of people.

## Chapter Three
# JUNE AVIS BRO

*June Avis Bro (1920-2019) found her life deeply affected by working with and having a reading from Edgar Cayce in 1943. She met Edgar Cayce through her future mother-in-law, Margueritte Harmon Bro, who had been asked to write a magazine review for Cayce's biography,* There Is a River. *Eventually, she and her husband, Harmon, moved to Virginia Beach to become members of the staff, witnessing many readings for themselves, becoming very close to Edgar and Gertrude Cayce and Gladys Davis. June often said that her time as a member of the Cayce household changed her life forever.*

*A graduate of Andover-Newton Theological School and the Chicago Theological Seminary, she taught on six campuses while raising five children. A concert pianist, counselor, pastor, and speaker, she had a background rich in the performing arts, Jungian studies, and the spiritual pilgrimage of women.*

*June shared memories of her experiences with Edgar Cayce in 2006, in honor of A.R.E.'s 75th anniversary.*

I listened skeptically as my new mother-in-law, Margueritte Harmon Bro, told the famous "Oil of Smoke" story, about how Edgar Cayce had prescribed, then located in the back room of a drugstore in another state, a bottle of medicine that had been recommended for a boy with a persistent leg sore. She had just returned from Virginia Beach and was full of enthusiasm about what she had experienced. I was planning a career in music and was not all that interested.

I had great respect for my mother-in-law, but how could I believe the stories she was telling? Edgar Cayce? Who was Edgar Cayce? Bach, Brahms, and Chopin were my world. My mother-in-law also reported that the manager of the Cayce work, Hugh Lynn Cayce, was now in the army overseas, and the Cayces needed help. They talked about the possibility of Harmon serving on the staff. Harmon's own Cayce reading revealed that he had once "worked with the sources of the information and should again." When Harmon's draft board approved of Harmon taking a year off from classes to do research with the Cayces at Virginia Beach, Harmon said he would like to go to Virginia Beach to explore the possibilities. Taken aback, I said that I needed time to think about it.

Once there, Harmon wrote me a letter. Reviewing it some sixty years later, I am amazed at how thoroughly he had grasped the scope, authenticity, and goodness of this work at the age of 23. Here are a few excerpts:

**October 26, 1943**
"I can't put into words my anxiety about whether you'll be willing to go to Virginia. In Chicago, you have a lovely little home, family, friends, time to practice. We eat well, have nice things and live with nice people. I'm asking you to very suddenly—in a week!—give up all the ties and move to a resort town that was just mud, drizzle, and hotels yesterday.

To make matters worse, we have many ties in the Chicago area. Neither of us has finished the graduate work we started—and worst of all, we will have to cancel the dates we have set up for presenting our musical program.

But every single objection you can make simply melts like tears when we see what the work out there does for people. Thin tubercular women, crippled boys, cancerous workmen, arthritic grandmothers knotted in pain—they all find healing. But that's only the beginning—what really happens to them is what has happened to Mr. and Mrs. Cayce, Gladys Davis, and some others—they find that "there is a river" of God's love flowing about us all, only waiting to be tapped by humble minds. The real miracles at Virginia Beach are the radiant, transformed lives, the people who go away realizing that they can actually find God and know Jesus and live like it. They say, "I am my brother's keeper " and their lives show it. They say, "There is only one God" and all their friends feel it. Buddhist, Muslim, Jew, Catholic, Mennonite, Christian Scientist, Humanist, Presbyterian—it goes on like the "Ballad for Americans"—they all find what they are searching for in the work of the readings and Mr. Cayce.

Don't think this is all sober business. I've laughed till I've ached during these last few days. These people who live so very sincerely seem just as near to the bubbling fountain of humor as they do to the well of eternal life. Mr. Cayce is just as much fun in his readings as he is out of them.

I could go on darling. But it gets me too excited, wondering whether you're going to knock me down or listen skeptically, or be annoyed, or thrilled, or all packed and ready to go—or what?"

I was all packed when he returned to Chicago! In fact, I packed so hastily, that I left my wedding dress. My landlady gave it to the Salvation Army.

We traveled to Virginia Beach by train, ferry, and taxi. The Cayces invited us to their home. Gladys was there, too. They showed us around, and took us into the office. They proudly pointed out the wild asparagus and the rows of strawberries in the nearby field.

Gladys showed us letters stacked knee-high around the main office. Thomas Sugrue's biography, *There Is a River*, and an article by my mother-in-law for *Coronet* magazine, "Miracle Man of Virginia Beach," had brought in so many requests for readings that Gladys had already scheduled them two years ahead. I could see plenty of work for willing hands.

One day, Edgar poked his head in the door where I sat typing and asked me if I'd like a reading. Of course, I wanted one, but didn't feel right about barging in ahead of those already booked. I'd seen the immense pain and life-threatening situations in those letters. "Mr. Cayce, you are my last hope! My child has an inoperable brain tumor!" "Mr. Cayce, my son is missing in action. Please find him!" "Mr. Cayce, please help. I am depressed and can't find any reason to go on." "Mr. Cayce I have a continual itch that cannot be scratched."

I suddenly felt guilty. Here I was, young and healthy with my whole life opening up in joyous, rich ways. I was relieved when Mr. Cayce assured me that it was customary for everyone on the staff to receive a reading.

When the moment came, my heart was pounding and my mind whirling! What would my reading say? Would it reveal selfishness and pettiness? Insecurities? Weird habits? Faults? Used and unused talents? Would he advise me to continue my music studies and aim for a professional career? Everyone in the office talked about reincarnation as though it was for sure. Although it was a new concept for me, I immediately felt that it made sense. Now I was wondering if I had ever been famous or especially helpful.

Mr. Cayce lay down, and loosened his tie and belt. Gertrude and Gladys made comments about funny things that had happened that day. Gertrude said she had made some karma for herself that morning when she'd gotten impatient with the grocer, Mr. Brothers. They did everything they could to make me feel at ease.

Mr. Cayce said a prayer and then took some deep breaths. Gertrude covered his eyes. After she gave the suggestions, Mr. Cayce began to speak in his normal voice, only a little more regulated and farther back in his throat.

The first thing he said was. "Yes, what a funny little body!" I had no idea what that meant. Was he seeing my good sense of humor or some strange weirdness? Mae St. Clair had helped me get my questions together. One of her readings from Mr. Cayce had saved her life after she had eaten some beans from her garden that had been sprayed with a toxic weed killer. She thought that was Mr. Cayce's way of saying that he thought I was cute! I decided to go with that.

Then Cayce said, "We have the records here of that entity now known as or called June Avis Bro. In giving the interpretation of the records as we find them, these we would choose from same with the desire and purpose that this information may prove a helpful experience for the entity." It was comforting to hear that Mr. Cayce's primary desire was to be helpful; not to shame, nor ridicule, nor admonish me.

Then a warning. He said, "Remember, God is not mocked, and whatsoever an individual sows, that must it also reap." He wanted me to know that every experience I had had so far, and those yet to come, were the fruits of my own actions along with the ideals I had held in one lifetime or another.

Then he zeroed in on my personality. "One who finds that when it meets individuals, it forms its opinion right now, and it is mighty hard to change." How true! I still size up people quickly, but I have been working hard on allowing myself to be pleasantly surprised.

He said, "In Venus, we find the appreciation of nature, and yet the entity doesn't hold very much to it." This was absolutely true. I do indeed love nature's beauties, smells, sounds, and creatures, but in the long run, I am a people person. I need people and music and culture. My musical talents and tastes came from sojourns in the Venus consciousness, he said. He also mentioned Mars and Jupiter, Mars being the consciousness in which energies are harnessed and put to work, and Jupiter where one learns that the universe is one. The Jupiter experience teaches a concern for the underdog, and what it means to be just, loving, and accepting. It wasn't that Cayce was suggesting that I had experienced lifetimes on these planets; instead, from Cayce's perspective the planets represented focused lessons in consciousness that had occurred in between earthly lifetimes.

Next, Mr. Cayce said that my life would be more harmonious and peaceful if my ideals corresponded with what God would have me do. He said, "You'll have a long list in the beginning, but eventually there will be just one." That one for me is Jesus.

Mr. Cayce emphasized not all incarnations would be given. He said I'd see patterns with certain variations, like a theme and variations in music. The older I get, the clearer I see those patterns and the ideals they cluster around. For me, these patterns relate first to making a home and family my career. Second, they

connect to using my musical talents creatively in the
home, and helping my husband in his work. Third, I
see my deep love for the church and church music.
Fourth, there is a pattern of my abiding love for God
and a feeling of awe at His endless, dazzling creativity.

Then Mr. Cayce repeated a phrase, "For as
indicated, ye enter not by chance but are chosen; then
use, do not abuse, the opportunities which are thine in
the journey through this experience."

It is hard to estimate how well I have done with
this challenge. It hasn't always been easy living up to
the guidance in my reading. Between the demands of
a large family and a husband who lived on the cutting
edge of ideas and communities, I often forgot that I
was here to learn about God's ways in the midst of
changes and demands.

Mr. Cayce then went into my past lives. He talked
about a lifetime in the Chicago area when it was
known as Fort Dearborn. Evidently, I found great
disturbances there during the French and Indian
Wars. I was allowed to stay because, according to the
reading, I was "able to make friends with both the
French and the Indians, and proved to be a helpful
influence." I connected with this incarnation in two
ways.

First, I have always had a soft spot in my heart
for Native Americans. As a child, I'd walk out of
the theater in the middle of a movie whenever I saw
Indians being mistreated. At the Girl Scout Camp I
attended when I was young, I spent most of my time
with a Native American called Gaw-Gee-Gaw-Bow,
as he sat whittling bows and arrows for our target
shooting. I loved hearing his stories.

Second, I have always loved anything French. For my
eightieth birthday, friends made a gift to me of a trip to

France. My visit felt like a homecoming after a long time away. Edgar Cayce's Source had scored a hit!

Then my reading cited an incarnation in the Holy Land when Paul and the disciples were building churches. Mr. Cayce said I was in the church at Laodicea, and when it threatened to split over differences in interpretations of Jesus' teachings, I tried to hold it together by psalm singing. Learning about this incarnation explained two deep passions: First, my love for the church, even though I can clearly see its weaknesses. It still seems to me that the church is the optimum community for keeping God in focus and meaning in our lives. I think my deep love of the church began in that incarnation in Laodicea. Second, my love of sacred music. I truly believe that singing helps resolve people's differences. In this incarnation, I am continually either singing in choirs or directing them. Cayce told me that for most of that incarnation, I gained, "bringing helpfulness to the work of the church through those areas."

Mr. Cayce cited an earlier experience with Joshua in the Holy Land as he set out to conquer Canaan. I was a sister of Rahab, whose family entertained the Israelite spies as they tried to get the lay of the land. Rahab hid them on her roof and when the walls of the city came down, she and her family were taken into the tribe of Judah. Mr. Cayce said that in the name then, Adjar, I learned "wonders, and trusts in the God, Yahweh, through the ministry of Joshua." When I was thirty-five, I had an experience that connected me with this incarnation.

I became utterly entranced by a TV movie about the biblical Ruth and Naomi and Naomi's kinsman, Boaz. I laughed and cried, and couldn't get it out of my mind for weeks. Ten years later, I was in seminary on my way to becoming a minister, studying the Gospel of

Matthew. I began with the first chapter, wishing I could skip the boring begat verses. When I read, "Salmon begat Boaz by Rahab," I blinked. I understood in a flash why I had gotten so caught up in Ruth's story. Boaz was my nephew, and undoubtedly I was at his wedding to Ruth, drinking, singing, praying, and celebrating.

My reading included an incarnation in Egypt in which I held a station in the Temple Beautiful, preparing women for motherhood and other home-building activities. I was an instructor in the "art of living, of caring for the body, of preparations for the varied activities in the earth."

At the time of my reading, my children were not yet born, but as I look back over the years, I realize that I have always been fascinated by motherhood. As a teen, I always enjoyed babysitting. And I remember giving birth to my own five children, wanting to know how every mother in the ward was doing. I was interested in each child in the nursery, and I found my own endlessly fascinating. Once my doctor and nurses didn't tell me that my roommate was unmarried and had to give her baby up for adoption. I kept asking her when the nurses were going to bring her baby to her, and why her husband hadn't come to see her. She always avoided me. On my last day in the hospital, the nurses told me the truth. I cried. My roommate couldn't have missed my own delight with the new child in my arms, and how happy I was when my husband visited. Out-of-wedlock babies were hush-hush in the fifties. I felt sad that I had made that young mother's life harder, and I grieved with her over the loss of the child she would never hold in her arms. My Temple Beautiful incarnation became a reality for me.

Here, in a nutshell, is what my reading did, and continues to do for me. First, it gave me an intimate, precise direction for this incarnation and at the same time gave me a long view of where my soul is headed. I don't have to ask myself whether I chose the right vocation. I know I did. "Do make the home the career for this is the greater career any may have in the earth. Those who shun same will have much yet to answer for. Use your abilities as in music to help your husband in his chosen profession." I may not have done it perfectly, but I entered into the work of building a home with all my heart, and I was thrilled to use my music working with my husband.

Second, it has laid to rest many fears, especially the fear of death. I don't have to wish I could be sure of life after death, I know. Like a family tree of past incarnations, my reading has established long lines of relationships to the primary people in my life. I know we will continue to meet and work on important issues. And I don't have to ask in desperation, who am I, or where am I going? I know.

Third, it has made me aware of limitations and temptations. When I asked Cayce whether Harmon and I should go to St. Olaf College to study the choral music that had brought us together, he said, "If the college will teach you how to entertain, forget it! If it teaches you how to build a home, do it!" Somewhere down the line of past lives, I had evidently deserted my family and been drawn into dancing and singing, probably as a nightclub entertainer in Jericho. Harmon and I were accepted at St. Olaf College, I took courses on how to use color and design in the home, and we both sang in the choir. As we sang, I felt certain that memories of the church in Laodicea were floating near.

Fourth, it warned me of a need to keep my husband "in line." He was intelligent, attractive, dynamic, and complex. Though we'd been married only a few months,

I knew it would be hard for me to keep up. I tried but didn't believe in myself enough. Harmon could be very persuasive, insistent, and assertive. He was a visionary and a reformer. When authorities couldn't see how valuable his suggestions might be, Harmon would feel dispirited and quit. We moved forty-seven times.

Fifth, my reading encourages me in difficult times. It reminds me of the words of Jesus, "If anyone gives so much as a cup of cold water to one of these little ones because he is a disciple, then I tell you most solemnly, he will most certainly not lose his reward." Mr. Cayce picked out this Bible verse especially for me and my whole being said, "Yes!" When the people close to me are being selfish or thoughtless, it urges me to make a response that will bring refreshment and healing. I remember the cool, sweet taste of water when I was berry picking with my Dad in Ironwood, Michigan, in the hot days of August, and feeling thirsty. In those days we could drink out of the cool stream nearby. The cup has become a touchstone symbol for me. When I bring it to mind, it immediately centers and quiets me. Then I can tune in to someone else's pain and willingly and lovingly offer that "cup of cold water."

My reading steered me toward what has brought my life's greatest fulfillment—the home and children. "You should have lots of little ones." Luckily, Harmon wanted them, too.

Every bit of information in my Cayce reading is precious to me. Sixty-three years have passed, and I am still stunned by the close fit of my reading. In the early years, I wished Mr. Cayce had given me lifetimes of world-famous personages who had once been me —people who had helped transform this world into something better, or who had given the world great gifts of music or pieces of art. But what came through, came straight from my soul and the traces I had left in the Akashic records. It showed me a picture of my soul's progress.

Not a day goes by that I do not feel the influence of Edgar Cayce's work. I was twenty-three when I went to Virginia Beach. For ten months, I was part of a courageous, God-directed, ground-breaking educational effort. The wisdom in the readings has shaped my life like nothing else except the Bible and the church. In the lyrics of a song by Stephen Sondheim:

> **Not a day goes by, not a single day, that you're not somewhere a part of my life. I keep thinking when does it end? That it can't get much better much longer.**
>
> **But it only gets better and stronger, and deeper and nearer, and simpler and freer, and richer and clearer, and no, not a day goes by, not a blessed day.**

The gratitude I feel has increased, not diminished, in more than sixty years. My Cayce reading set before me the reason I came into the earth at this time. The Source knew me better than I knew myself—my inner being, my persona, my childhood, my idiosyncrasies, my past lives, my weaknesses, and my reason for being. Later, my insights and self-discoveries have shown how snugly my reading fits. It warms me like a beautiful, expensive coat that never gets threadbare and never goes out of style.

## Chapter Four

# LUCILLE KAHN

*Lucille Kahn (1902-1995) was an actress when she first met Edgar Cayce in 1924 through David Kahn, whom she later married.* A *young New York business entrepreneur, David had been a close friend of Edgar Cayce's since he was a teenager and had been invited to assist at a Cayce reading for one of the Kahn's neighbors.*

*It was in great part due to David and Lucille's support in the early days that Cayce and his work became known to many prominent and influential people. The Kahns both served on the A.R.E. Board of Directors, and Lucille was president from 1967 to 1969.*

*David Kahn died in 1968, shortly before the publication of his book,* My Life with Edgar Cayce. *Lucille remained active with the A.R.E. until her own death in 1995. This interview is a compilation of interviews in the 1960s and in 1984 and 1985.*

I was playing at the Belasco Theater in New York in 1924 in "Laugh Clown Laugh," starring Lionel Barrymore. One evening, I received a note backstage from a man named David Kahn asking me if I was the Miss Kahn (my family name was also Kahn— no relation to David's family) who was a member of the

Dreyfus family of Tulsa, Oklahoma. Mutual friends had asked that he look me up.

I invited him to dinner with my sister and me. We had not been together very long when he began to talk about a man named Edgar Cayce, who, he said, could go into a sleep state or trance and diagnose physical ailments and who talked about former lives and how we carry over tendencies and talents.

I was born in 1902, and I had never heard of reincarnation, karma, mysticism, or any of these philosophies. I looked at David and wondered, "What in the world have I picked up here?" My sister and I found him fascinating but did not believe a word he said! But we were able to check out one of his stories about meeting some of our relatives and found it was true. We thought maybe he was telling the truth, and we continued to see each other.

After "Laugh Clown Laughed" closed, I got the lead opposite Otis Skinner in "Sancho Panza," which went on the road. The Cayces were then living in Dayton, Ohio, and Dave urged me to invite them to see the play so we could meet. Edgar and his wife Gertrude came backstage afterwards, and Edgar said they had enjoyed the show very much. I said, "I'm glad you did and now I want to see your show."

The next morning, I went to their home and witnessed my first reading. It was for a child who could not keep any food down. The doctors had tried everything they knew and the parents, in desperation, had turned to Edgar Cayce for a reading. In the reading, Cayce suggested that the child be put on a diet for the time being of nothing but ripe bananas.

I was outraged! I thought that the baby would die and that this man should be turned in for practicing medicine without license. I left the house really indignant. It worried me so much that I followed up on the case. To my surprise, I learned that the child was doing very well.

Meanwhile, Dave suggested that I get a life reading, which he said would tell me about my past incarnations and their influence on the present. In part, the reading said, "In the mental forces, we find one well adapted to the present conditions and endeavors; one capable of going much higher in the dramatic elements of the profession . . ."

One of the questions we asked was whether I could be a successful actress if I married a businessman. I also wanted to know if I would be content if I renounced my career for marriage. This was the answer:

> **The body, mentally and spiritually capable of renouncing career for another career, establishing and making a home, the greater career an individual can make in an earth's plane, for it becomes a pattern of that sort before the inmost of every entity. This individual must decide that for self. These are the possibilities, the qualifications, for the entity to make a success from either; not possible to make both . . .**

There I was playing the lead opposite Otis Skinner – what did I want with a home and cooking and babies? Nothing could have interested me less just then!

I finished the tour and continued to see a great deal of David Kahn. I was having a bad season—absolutely nothing was happening with my career. I was not right for any part. I used to tease Dave and one day said, "I've never played a wife before. Maybe this is the time to do so?" That is how I finally accepted his proposal of marriage.

We spent part of our honeymoon visiting the Cayces who had moved to Virginia Beach, and it soon became clear that I had married not only David Kahn but the entire Cayce family!

I loved Edgar Cayce. He was a tall, slim man with a great drawl, a high forehead, the bluest eyes I have ever seen, and this sweet gentle manner—always courteous and very patient. If I had cast a Cayce movie then, I would have cast the young Jimmy Stewart as Edgar Cayce and Eddie Albert as my husband Dave.

Mr. Cayce was a marvelous cook. He made peach preserves and fig preserves. He had planted fig trees that were growing beautifully; he really had a green thumb.

I always remember him sitting out on a little pier over a pond near their house, fishing or whittling with his pocketknife. He had planted a weeping willow tree in a floating, wooden drum. The drum had a rope attached to it so that when it got too hot he would pull in the willow tree to give him shade.

Dave always called Edgar Cayce "Judge," because when he was young it would have been disrespectful to call him "Edgar," and "Mr. Cayce" seemed too formal and remote. He felt that Edgar Cayce would judge his life by the same high standards Cayce applied to his own.

One day, Judge invited me to attend the Sunday school class he taught. Mr. Cayce was a fine teacher. Afterwards he remarked that it was certainly a full house. I said, "Judge, it was well attended but by no means a full house. I don't understand you."

"Oh," he said, "I'm talking about my invisible friends—discarnate entities. They were all there today. The place was filled."

Dave and I settled into a large New York apartment

after our honeymoon. We invited the Cayces and Gladys Davis, who took down and transcribed all the readings, to come stay with us for a month in the spring and again in the fall. Mr. Cayce was not yet well known, and we thought this would be a good chance to introduce him to people and arrange for them to have readings. We would invite friends the first night; the next night those friends would invite their friends, and so on.

Mr. Cayce could only give two readings a day, so he would make appointments to give more readings after he returned to Virginia Beach. This would keep him busy for some months, after which they would come to New York again, and we would have another round of invitations.

Dave was devoted to Judge. He spent about half of every day of his life talking to people about Edgar Cayce. Dave had the reputation of being a very astute businessman but he was just absolutely fixated on the subject of Cayce. If he had not been so successful, his business associates would have thought him suspect. He had his feet on the ground, so they tolerated this eccentricity.

One of Dave's life readings indicated that he had served Cayce before, during Cayce's incarnation as a high priest in ancient Egypt named Ra Ta. They had been brought together again. This time, Dave wanted to make Edgar Cayce's name known all over the world, and to be helpful to those who came to him.

A very happy time for all of us was when the hospital was being built. Morton Blumenthal had been getting readings on the stock market. He had promised that he would buy that property at the beach and build that hospital. And he kept that promise. It was agreed that Dave would furnish it, and all of Cayce's other friends would make the contributions that they could make.

I recall, almost every Friday night, Morton and his wife, Adeline, and Dave and I would take a boat from New York, go down the Chesapeake Bay, arrive in Norfolk, Virginia, in the morning and drive out to the beach. There with Judge, we would see the hospital going up. I think Judge supervised every nail that went into that place, and his heart was in it. It was a very happy time for all of us. Afterwards, the four of us would go back to New York.

Morton had now become a real student of psychical research and metaphysics, and he was totally absorbed with dream interpretation. He began to have a series of very troublesome dreams, and on one occasion he called Judge to get a reading on a dream—he didn't like the dream he had had. So the reading came back and in so many words it said to get out of the stock market. Judge had also told Dave to get out of the market. And I remember one night the two of them, Dave and Morton, discussed it. They said, "You know the market is at an all-time high; the country has never been so affluent. Judge is simply off timewise." But he wasn't. the Crash came, and most of us were wiped out.

I remember the morning that the Hospital closed, the last morning. Dave and I with Judge were all standing at the foot of this high dune—the hospital was built on the highest spot in Virginia Beach, facing the ocean. The sun was shining in Judge's eyes. They were blue, and they were moist with tears, and he said, "Dave, look at that building. No matter what they try to do with it, it will never succeed unless it is used for the purpose for which it was built." It ended up being exactly what happened.

During their visit to New York in the fall of 1931, the Cayces and Gladys Davis stayed at a hotel where they gave readings. Two ladies living in the hotel called

Gladys and said they were desperate to have a reading. Gladys said they were completely booked but she would call if there should be a cancellation. Gladys also told them about the A.R.E. and gave them a membership application. One of the women applied, and paid her dues in order to be eligible for a reading. There was a cancellation the next day and she received a reading. After it was over and Mr. Cayce woke up, she arrested the Cayces for fortune telling.

Dave was out of town when I got the call that the Cayces had been taken to jail. I called an attorney—a friend who was close to the Cayce work—and asked him to go down and do whatever he could for them. When the case came to trial, Dave appeared as a witness for the defense. The case was eventually dismissed; here is an excerpt from the magistrate's summary from the trial transcript:

**After seeing the people's witnesses and the three defendants and their witness on the stand, and observing their manner of testifying, and after reading the exhibits in the case, I find as a fact that Mr. Cayce and his co-defendants were not pretending to tell fortunes, and that to hold these defendants guilty ... would be an interference with the belief, practice, or usage of an incorporated ecclesiastical governing body [A.R.E.], or the duly licensed teachers thereof, and they are discharged.**

Even though it was dismissed, it was a dreadful experience for those lovely people. To this day, I still wonder why the reading did not give some warning that these women — or the one who actually had the reading — were up to something, and say that the reading could not be given. I still have not answered that question.

Now the Depression is on. The Roosevelts are in the White House. The New Deal is on. Dave gets a reading and it said to write Mrs. Roosevelt, offer her your services in this critical period, and particularly that dealing with Arthurdale. Now we had never heard of Arthurdale, no one we knew had ever heard of Arthurdale, Judge had never heard of Arthurdale, but Dave writes Mrs. Roosevelt and she invites us to come out to her Hyde Park cottage. And then she tells us about this place. She said that in the Appalachian area, in West Virginia, these miners and their families were literally starving. The mines had closed.

The government had bought this land; each man had been given an acre of land where they were able to grow their food. There was a community farm. There was a chicken farm. There was an inn. And one of the things that Dave had to do was to bring in some industry so that these miners would learn something else. So he brings in radio cabinets. The miners were taught how to build these cabinets, and the wives were taught how to rub them down to a fine finish. I must say this was one of the most ennobling experiences that any group of people could possibly have.

In Virginia Beach, Mr. Cayce gave his readings in his study: a quiet room furnished with a long couch, a few chairs, and a desk. The walls were filled with pictures he had taken as a photographer. When giving a reading, Mr. Cayce would unlace his shoes, open his belt and his collar, stretch out on the couch, take a deep breath, and look up at the ceiling. Then, as his eyes began to flicker, Gertrude would give the suggestion, "You have before you the body of so and so, etc." At the end of the reading, there would be questions. This was in the days before tape recorders, so Gladys took everything down in shorthand, then transcribed it.

The life readings interested me the most. My first reading said that I had been in the theater in ancient Greece and Rome where I had given much joy to many people through my arts, dancing, and drama. Now that interested me very much because it helped to answer some questions that went way back about how I got into theater.

I had started out to be a violinist and studied at the Chicago Musical College, but I was never comfortable with the idea. One day, I went to the head of the college and asked if I could take dramatic arts classes in place of my violin classes. He agreed. Almost immediately, I seemed to know what to do on stage. A producer, Warren Wade, saw me in my first school play and offered me the ingénue role in his touring stock company. After several years with the stock company, I came to New York and immediately was engaged for the dream of my dreams: a role in "Laugh Clown Laugh," with Lionel Barrymore. Next came the lead opposite Otis Skinner in "Sancho Panza."

This did not make any sense to me before. I had not been able to understand how I just seemed to know how to act on stage. The Cayce reading provided a rational explanation for this, by indicating that we carry over certain talents from previous lives. I like a wonderful quote from Plato's "Theory of Reminiscence" about that, "Knowledge easily acquired is that which the enduring self had in an earlier life, so that it flows back easily."

In later readings, Mr. Cayce advised me about raising our two sons and said my part was to foster their spiritual development. When each of the two boys was a few months old, we had readings for them. The eldest, David, was told that he had been a doctor in many of his incarnations, and could be so again, if he so willed. The readings always emphasized "that which

you will to do." You were given a choice: you could
do so if you applied yourself. While there was never
any insistence from us that David go into medicine,
he decided to study at Harvard Medical School, and at
Columbia Psychoanalytic Institute, and became a gifted
psychoanalyst. In a reading for our younger son, Richard,
we were told he could and should be encouraged to go
into law. Today, he is a prominent attorney, working on
a national level. Both sons have served on the Board of
the American Society for Psychical Research. Richard,
formerly on the board, brought a profound interest in
metaphysics; and David, currently serving, combines
his traditional medical training in psychiatry with many
years as a researcher of paranormal powers.

While we all have many incarnations, Mr. Cayce
concentrated in his life readings on those incarnations
that would most significantly contributed to the present
lifetime. When my first child was born, and to outward
appearances I was most involved in childrearing, I
was simultaneously reconnecting with an important
previous incarnation and preparing myself for the work
that would occupy my future.

To regain my strength after David's birth, I began
to study yoga with a Sikh yogi, Dr. Baghat Thind. The
yoga exercises, which have been an integral part of my
daily practice ever since, led me to an intensive study of
Eastern philosophies. To clarify my strong affinity for
the East, I had what was called a "check" reading with
Mr. Cayce to see if individuals in my life today were
part of past incarnations. It seems I had been associated
with Edgar Cayce before, in an Indian incarnation, and
also with Dr. Baghat Thind, who had been my teacher
then too. According to the reading, in that lifetime I
coordinated Egyptian with Indian teachings and it was
then that my greatest spiritual unfoldment took place.

After observing many life readings, which demonstrated how people carried over talents and gifts, I wanted to understand more about these matters. I enrolled in a course in parapsychology, which was offered by Dr. Gardner Murphy at the New School for Social Research. Dr. Murphy was head of the department of psychology at Columbia University and later became president of the American Society for Psychical Research. Although the class was primarily for professionals, when I told Dr. Murphy of my experiences with Edgar Cayce and my desire to study these phenomena, he accepted me into the class.

Sometime later, I was asked to plan and conduct a lecture series for the A.R.E. group in New York. I was able to draw upon the learned scientists and doctors I had met in Dr. Murphy's class, as well as to invite prominent personal friends involved in the newly developing study of parapsychology. It was the first time that many of these eminent scientists had agreed to publicly discuss their interest in parapsychology.

This successful lecture series lasted twenty years, from 1954 to 1974. Lecturers included such internationally renowned figures as Gerald Heard, former BBC science commentator and brilliant scholar; Gertrude Schmeidler, noted parapsychologist and professor at city college in New York; Ian Stevenson, noted University of Virginia investigator of past-life memories; and C.J. Ducasse of Brown University, whose studies of Bridey Murphy brought scientific exactitude to the study of reincarnation.

One day, Hugh Lynn Cayce said to me, "Lucille, nothing like this is happening anywhere else. It's a showcase. You know, you are doing what you did once before. Your reading said you combined and coordinated the work of Egypt and India, and now you are doing that again through your studies in metaphysics, yoga, the Cayce work, and these lectures. Once again, you're acting as a catalyst." Thus, I experienced in my own life how activities of the past effect our present and help us to shape our future.

I owe the Cayce readings a great deal. They laid out a road map for me, and I found I could depend on it. It was true to the nature of my need. I think everything is there for people if they want to make the effort to study it, use it, and live it intentionally.

The Edgar Cayce story is most eloquently expressed in Tom Sugrue's definitive biography, *There Is a River*. Perhaps Tom's inscription in my copy of his book best epitomizes the commitment and involvement of all of us who knew, admired, and loved Edgar Cayce:

> *To David and Lucille. This story, in which we lived, and which lived in us, is ended now — but all that it taught must go on — that is our obligation, our trust and our privilege — it is our meaning.*

# Chapter Five
# DAVID E. KAHN

*David E. Kahn (1893-1968) was born in Kentucky and introduced to Edgar Cayce when he was a teenager. The two began a lifelong friendship. His enthusiasm for the Cayce work was unsurpassed. In fact, Gladys Davis Turner, Edgar Cayce's secretary, estimated that David Kahn had referred, either directly or indirectly, at least one-half of all of the individuals who obtained readings from Edgar Cayce!*

*Dave saw Cayce as a friend, a mentor and advisor, and he gave Cayce the nickname, "Judge." Over the years, Dave would have more than 200 readings of his own, on every imaginable topic: dreams, business advice, health, relationships, and personal direction.*

*When Edgar Cayce's biography,* There Is a River, *was published, Cayce dedicated it, as follows: "To Dave, whose friendship has often helped over the troubled path, as well as lightened the burden of others."*

*This is a compilation of two interviews that occurred in the 1960s.*

When I was a teenager in Lexington, Kentucky, our next door neighbor, Mr. Delaney, invited a psychic to come to Lexington to help his wife, who was critically ill. His wife was crippled, and partially paralyzed. She was in a wheelchair, and couldn't even comb her hair or take care of herself. Mr. Cayce had been asked to come see if he could help her using his psychic ability. I was asked by Mr. Delaney to come over and be of whatever help I could. I was thrilled to be invited to such an occasion.

I remember when he got there, Mr. Delaney asked, "Do you want to see my wife and talk to her?"

Cayce said, "No, there's nothing I can do when I'm awake. They tell me when I'm asleep, I'm able to help people. After the reading, I'd like to meet her."

He then turned to me and said, "Would you take down the reading?"

I said, "Well, if you tell me how." I had never seen anything like this before, and it was really an occasion because I felt like this was going to prove very important in my life.

He handed me a little black book and he said, "Now, as I lie on the floor and get ready to give this reading, I want you to read these suggestions. I will place myself in the proper condition and I want you to read this suggestion and I will go to sleep. As I give the reading, I want you write down what I say as best you can. When I am finished, I will ask you to give me any questions, and then you can give me the suggestion to wake up." He pointed out what I was supposed to read aloud and when to do it.

He went to sleep on the floor and I gave the suggestion. He described Mrs. Delaney's condition from head to foot, giving the temperature and blood pressure and all the things that a doctor would normally do. I was amazed at how definite he was in talking about somebody he'd never even seen. He described where the condition had started, what the condition was now, and what needed to be done with an osteopath, as well as a massage, and a prescription.

A couple of times I didn't know how to spell a word, and I asked him to spell it and he'd spell it right off. Any question I asked him, he'd answer immediately. This was all amazing to me. He continued for about forty or forty-five minutes and then said, "We are through with this reading."

I thought he had given a wonderful reading. I then read the suggestion he had told me to, something like, "There will be no ill effects to your body. You'll take on none of the conditions of the patient. You will wake up normally, feeling perfectly fine in every respect." About a minute later, his eyes opened, and he got up. This tall, lanky country boy had now become a very important doctor to me.

I was so thrilled over the situation that I wanted to follow through. I went down immediately to the drugstore with this prescription. I didn't know these words or the medicines — there were about ten of them. I called on the local druggist, Mr. William Dunn, and I asked him if he'd heard of these things. He said he could put them together. So I waited and I got the bottle, and I brought it back to Mr. Delaney.

In the meantime, we had to find an osteopath. I had never heard of an osteopath before. I didn't know what they did. But Delaney found an osteopath and they began the treatments and the medication within a day or so.

About five or six days later, Mr. Delaney asked me to come over. He said, "I want to see you my wife."

Well, I went over there and she was a mess. She had red spots breaking out all over from what looked like the top of her head to her toes. They believe that the prescription had something to do with this, so they sent for the doctor who lived next door to me.

The doctor wasn't happy. Apparently, Mr. Delaney had spoken to him earlier about calling Cayce because he said, "I want no part of this because I don't know what caused it. I was against this Cayce fellow in the first place and now you've gotten into it."

After that, I suggested to Mr. Delaney that we send Cayce a telegram. It simply said, "Please inform us now, what is the condition of the patient, and what we shall we do next?"

A telegram came back. Cayce took another reading in Hopkinsville. He said, "If you do what you are told to do, you will get the results as promised." He went on to say that the druggist had filled the prescription wrong — one of the ingredients was apparently missing. He said that black sulfur was missing from the prescription.

So I went back to meet with the druggist and asked him if he had included the black sulfur. He said, "I never heard of black suffer, so I put sulfur in there; otherwise, it's exactly as written. I don't know where you could get black sulfur."

So, I decided to wire Mr. Cayce, "Where can we find black sulfur?"

Next day or so, we got a telegram back, apparently he had taken another reading and it said, "Parke-Davis, Detroit, Michigan."

Well, it took us several days but eventually we had the right prescription, the osteopath, and the massages. These were all followed as the reading had suggested. Mrs. Delaney got well. She could comb her own hair. She no longer had to use the wheelchair. She took care of herself. I often saw her get into her car and go where she pleased.

After that, my whole family got involved with the readings. Cayce and I became lifelong friends; I called him "Judge." My mother had readings that were so helpful she once told me, "We've got to do whatever we can to help this man."

The readings have been a part of my whole life—business advice, health, personal advice—all kinds of help. I was raised in the grocery business and the readings suggested I should go into the army before war was declared. The readings guided me into the wood, metal, and furniture business. They suggested I relocate to New York, rather than Kentucky, after the war, which I did. That's where I met my wife. They gave guidance for both of my sons. In fact, the older boy was saved from having to be delivered by Caesarean because of the readings. When my mother got very sick, the doctor told her she wouldn't live five days. We got a reading and she got well. In fact, she outlived the doctor for seven years because of the advice given in the readings.

My own life reading proved to be very helpful to my business in an interesting way. Judge told me that I had lived during the American Revolution and had been on the British side, until the war ended and then I decided to stay, becoming involved in trade. While the war was occurring I was an aid to the British General William Howe, keeping open supply chains on the American side, as well as in Montreal and Quebec. The reading went on to say that I could have a very positive working relationship with General Brehon Somervell, who was responsible for U.S. Army logistics. He had been responsible for the construction of a number of WPA construction projects and was head of the construction division of the Quartermaster Corps. Cayce said that Somervell had, in fact, been General Howe during the Revolutionary War.

Well, the next time I had the opportunity to have lunch with Mrs. Roosevelt, I told her one of the people I would most like to meet was General Somervell. Somervell was essentially head of supplies for the entire U.S. Army. The introduction was eventually made and for me it was just like an instant recognition. We hit it off immediately. I explained that I was responsible for Brunswick Radio and Television; eventually I supplied the army with all kinds of supplies through my relationship with Somervell. We had a great working relationship and it was certainly an enormous boost to my business. The whole time I knew him, he treated me with kindness, faith, and complete confidence. I think we picked up our relationship exactly where we had left it off.

One of my favorite stories has to do with Colonel William Starling, who worked for the White House Secret Service and was ready to retire. Starling was from Kentucky and had been in school with Judge back in Hopkinsville. Starling had worked in the Secret Service for seven Presidents, beginning with Teddy Roosevelt and ending with Franklin Roosevelt: Roosevelt, Taft, Wilson, Harding, Coolidge, Hoover, and Roosevelt.

I was working with the President and Mrs. Roosevelt at Arthurdale, West Virginia, from one of these camps during the Depression and that brought me to the White House very often. One day, Starling said to me, "I'm going to retire and I've spoken to the President about it; I want you to handle my book."

I said, "Well there are plenty of newspaper people around here."

And he said, "No, I want you to handle it."

I said, "Bill, I'm not an author, I'm not a publisher. I've never done any writing of any kind. The only way I would undertake such an important thing in your life is to have you go to Virginia Beach with me and meet your old friend, Cayce, and if he gives a reading and he tells me what to do, I will do it. Otherwise, I wouldn't dare touch it; I haven't the ability for it."

Well, he picked up the telephone right then and there and made the appointment for a private car to Norfolk.

We arrived the next day and nobody was more surprised than Edgar Cayce.

When we walked in unannounced, he said, "Bill what are you doing here?"

He said, "Well this crazy guy here will not talk about my book unless you advise him."

With that, four or five bags of mail came in that day because there had appeared in *Coronet* magazine the story of the "Miracle Man of Virginia Beach," and Judge was standing there with a pen knife opening up the mail—queries from all over America.

We sat down and talked a few minutes. Afterwards, we went back into the room, took off his collar and tie, lay on his back, and we made the suggestion. And the reading on the book was given in about forty-five minutes. He told us at that the book would be a good book if it was done on a sweet basis, not getting into politics but dealing with the home life of the President, Mrs. Roosevelt, and their children, and conditions around the nation, and covering his thirty years in the White House, pertaining to the seven Presidents from Teddy to Franklin.

Then we asked a lot of questions about when the book should come out, who should publish it, who should write it. I asked how many would sell, and he said it would be 100,000 or more. Well, 10,000 is a usual good book, 20,000 is exceptional, and this, of course, was fantastic. The questions that were asked, he'd answer them just as fast and we would ask them.

The thing that amazed me was that we had a successful book in *There Is a River*—Henry Holt Publishing Company—and he turns us into Simon & Schuster, of whom I heard but didn't know. Well, I thought that was unusual.

When he woke up, I said, "Judge, what is this, you take us away from Henry Holt after a successful book and deliver us to Simon & Schuster?"

He said, "Who are they?"

I said, "Well they're quite an important publishing house in New York but I don't know them."

We spent the day there and we returned then to Washington. I said goodbye to Bill and I came on to New York and caught the only taxicab in Pennsylvania Station that was standing there at one o'clock in the morning with 1,000 people standing around. I looked over and saw a man in the back of the crowd with a big suitcase on his shoulder. I said, "You over there, with the big suitcase. Are you going up town?" I was embarrassed. All these people—one person, two people in a cab.

"Sure," he said. "I'm going up town and I'd like to ride." I said, "Come on over."

He gets in, puts down his coat, puts down his suitcase. He says, "Schuster's my name."

I said, "You wouldn't be of Simon & Schuster?"

He says, "I'm Maxwell Schuster."

I said, "I'm David E. Kahn, and you're going to publish a book for me."

He said, "What book?"

I said, "Starling of the White House."

He said, "Bill Starling? Well, how does he come to you?"

"Well he comes to me because I had a psychic down in Virginia Beach yesterday, Edgar Cayce . . .," and then I told him the story how the reading was given.

He might have been thinking I was crazy or a lunatic but he asked, "Is the book written?"

I said, "Not yet."

He asked, "Who's going to write it?" I said, "Thomas Sugrue."

Well, he said, "Tom works for me. He was a ghostwriter for Craig's *Danger Is my Business*, and a good writer.

"Well," I said, "Tom doesn't know about it yet, because we only got this information yesterday, you're going to publish the book though . . ."

I said goodbye to Mr. Schuster, and he asked, "When does Starling come to town?"

I said, "He'll be here Wednesday."

I called Bill and he came in, and Quincy Howell, Dick Simon, Mr. Schuster, and myself had lunch, and the book then was decided upon. We then left for Clearwater Beach, Florida, where Tom Sugrue was living with his wife and child, Patsy. My wife, Lucille, accompanied us. And Starling, Lucille, and I sat on the beach and discussed the book with Tom. Starling would write all of his references on a yellow pad, and Tom would then transcribe it into his book.

After the book was written, they tell me, that every time Monday morning came, Max Schuster would say, "How's the Cayce book coming?" He'd hear back: 10,000, 20,000, 40,000, finally 100,000 was reached, and one day I saw in *The New York Times* a full page article of "How a Bestseller Is Born." "Mr. S of S & S" — that's Mr. Schuster of Simon and Schuster — "stated that he met a mysterious stranger coming in from Washington, who told him of a psychic named Edgar Cayce of Virginia Beach, who had given a reading on the kind of book and all of the details of the book about Starling. This stranger had given his impression of the book. This had seven woodcuts of the seven Presidents around," and here was the story of Max Schuster, quoting what I had said of Cayce.

Eventually, the book sold over 200,000 copies. I think that's pretty good.

## Chapter Six
# EDGAR EVANS CAYCE

*Edgar Evans Cayce (1918-2013) was the youngest son of Edgar and Gertrude Cayce. His earliest recollection of being helped by his psychic father was a physical reading when he was seven years old and was treated for a serious burn that extended from his ankle all the way up his back.*

*The author of four books about his father's amazing psychic talent, he was an expert resource on Atlantis. He was frequently asked to describe what it was like having a psychic for a father, to which his reply was that having a psychic for a father wasn't all that different. He described Edgar Cayce as being a loving husband and father, a great gardener, a very good carpenter, an enthusiastic fisherman, and someone who could talk to anybody.*

*This interview occurred in 2006 in honor of A.R.E.'s 75th anniversary. The year also marked the 50th anniversary of buying back the Edgar Cayce Hospital building, which had been lost during the Depression.*

When A.R.E. was formed, I was thirteen years old. I was thirty-eight when the hospital was bought back. The Association of National Investigators had been the organization that preceded A.R.E. When the hospital closed its doors, my dad, Edgar

Cayce, was really at a low point in his life. You know, the hospital had been his dream. Prior to the hospital closing, the medical director, Dr. Thomas House, who was also Dad's friend, died as well. I think that Dad felt like everything he had hoped for had suddenly gone down the drain.

After the hospital closed, I remember Dad telling me that the building would never be a success at anything but what it had been intended for, and he was right. Over time, some of the best businessmen in Virginia Beach acquired the property. They tried to make it a motel. They tried to make it a nightclub. Over a period of years, they tried to make it half a dozen things. Eventually, the North End of Virginia Beach started to boom. The Ramada was built on 57th Street. Everything on the beach was booming, but nobody could do a thing with the old hospital. Finally, when it came up for sale, many A.R.E. people and study groups came together to help buy it back for about a hundred thousand dollars. Now keep in mind, the A.R.E. did not have enough money to pay the interest on the loan, but somehow we got it back, and it has been a success ever since. Dad was right about it succeeding for what it was intended.

What I remember most about the time after the hospital closed was that we had to move two or three times. For a time, we even lived right across the street from the old hospital, which I'm sure was really hard on Dad. Eventually we moved down to Arctic Circle by the lake and rented two little, tiny houses. My folks had to get two of them to have an office, as well as a place for the family and a place for Gladys Davis. We lived there a year or so before we were able to buy a place right across from the Catholic Church. That became Association headquarters and Dad lived there until he died.

Gladys Davis was just like a member of the family, and she had a memory like a computer. She could remember people's names and when they had readings. She'd remember their readings, when they'd written, what had been in their letters, and so forth. She also remembered Dad's letters because she had seen the letters that had been written back and forth. Dad wrote a lot of letters. He had an old Remington typewriter, and he had literally worn some of the lettering off of the keys. Gladys could remember so many things about people because she was there when the people were there, when the readings had taken place. She was amazing.

When we first came to Virginia Beach, I don't think there were six houses between 31st Street and the end of the North End. Laskin Road hadn't been built. All that existed was sand dunes between here and Cape Henry. We used to go up there and pick grapes—great big things that Dad used to make jelly and wine. You could pick them by the bushel.

Virginia Beach was just a tiny little fishing village then. Virginia Beach hadn't incorporated Princess Anne yet; it was just a strip of land along the oceanfront.

I remember there used to be a company at the oceanfront called Storemont's Fishing Company. They used to have these long wooden poles up out of the ocean with nets between them to catch fish. Sometimes during a storm, those poles would break off and drift ashore. We were so poor that my brother, Hugh Lynn, and I used to gather up those broken pieces of wood and saw them up for firewood for the fireplace. They burned real pretty because they were full of the ocean salts. Some of them would be green, red, blue, all colors. We sawed many a cord of wood from the oceanfront.

There used to be a train track that ran along Pacific Avenue. A lot of the railroad people used to come down here. They'd take a Pullman car down to the beach and park where the Cavalier Hotel is now. The train used to bring picnickers from Norfolk down to the old casino that used to be quite popular. Of course, it was illegal at the time but the city just looked the other way. One of my jobs used to be parking cars at the casino. We used to have some of the famous Big Bands down here, like Glenn Miller and his orchestra. The beach also used to have one theater. It was 10 cents to go see a movie but nobody had 10 cents in those days.

Virginia Beach started annexing property and eventually merged with Princess Anne County in 1963. That is when the city really started to grow. Virginia Beach is now the largest city in the state, with about a half million people.

I have often been asked what it was like having a psychic for a father. To tell you the truth, when I was real little, I used to think that everybody's father gave readings. I didn't know the difference. Growing up with it is different than coming into it from the outside because I used to watch him give readings. When I got older, I had readings myself. Over the years, I saw the readings work for many, many people, including my mother, my father, my brother, and myself. I had physical readings and life readings. As I grew up, I learned not to talk about it at school. Most of the people at the beach thought Dad was a doctor of some kind. They used to call him "Doc Cayce." When he would take me into the barbershop to get a haircut when I was little, they'd say, "How ya doing, Doc?"

One time during a reading, I asked where I should go to college, and it suggested Duke University. It suggested engineering and stated that I could get a scholarship. Well, I graduated from Oceana High School with twenty-eight people in the graduating class, and getting a scholarship to Duke seemed like the chance of a snowball in hell. Well, I put in for a scholarship and got a scholarship for my first year. I was valedictorian of the Oceana graduating class but still it was a small, small school.

My girlfriend, Kathryn "Kat" had a reading. She always kids me about it and says that if Dad hadn't recommended marriage for the two of us, we wouldn't have gotten married. Dad said that we had been associated before. This year, we will have been married sixty-three years!

One of the subjects that I really took an interest in came about in the early 1960s, after Dad had died. I was skeptical like anybody would have been about Atlantis because most people thought Atlantis was a myth. I decided to read every reading on Atlantis and see if I could find anything that might prove it. I thought I would go down to A.R.E. at night and read all the readings that mentioned Atlantis. I figured the project would take me a few weeks. At the time, all of the readings were on microfilm that could be viewed through one of those roller-type machines. There was no index system yet, so I had to scroll through all of the life readings. The project I had thought would take a month took me over a year. I worked for two or three nights a week, maybe two or three hours a night, and finally read through every one of them.

As I read the readings on Atlantis, I made notes and tried to organize it into time periods and subjects. Dad didn't often give dates, you know, unless somebody asked him. But a few were mentioned, so I tried to group the readings into one of the three destructions he spoke about. One occurring around 50,000 B.C., when the first part of Atlantis was submerged; another occurring about 28,000 B.C., when they had the second destruction and the continent was split into islands; and the last one about 10,000 B.C., when the last islands went down. The final destruction is the one that Plato talked about.

Dad made statements in some of these Atlantis readings that later proved to be accurate. For example, he was talking about this ray that they had in Atlantis and the technology that they had reached. He said that this would be discovered in twenty-five years. Well, almost exactly twenty-five years later, the Bell laboratories discovered the laser.

Dad also talked about humankind being in the earth a lot longer than geology and archaeology claimed to be true. Most of the early readings were in the 1920s and 1930s at a time when science believed humans had inhabited North America for two or three thousand years at most. Dates of 10,000 or 20,000 years or longer were ridiculous. We now know that carbon dating suggests humans have been in places much longer than was supposed. Over the years, it's turned out that people lived in the places Dad said they had at the time he said they did.

In the past, no one believed that the poles had ever shifted. Now there is real good evidence that they have shifted before. They've found mammals in Siberia that are frozen with tropical vegetation in their stomach. All the things that he said about the past have been proven accurate with recent discoveries.

Later on, Hugh Lynn and I wrote a book about those occasions when Dad might not have been completely accurate. It is called *The Outer Limits of Edgar Cayce's Power*. The two of us wanted to look at those occasions when the readings seemed to have been wrong. In all, perhaps 200 out of the 14,000 could have been somewhat inaccurate—now that's still a pretty good batting average. It gives him about a 98 or 99 percent accuracy rate. In the end, I came to the conclusion that there were explainable reasons why some of these readings were wrong.

You see, overall there are probably four sources of psychic information evidenced in the Cayce files. One of them, of course, is the unconscious memory of everything you ever read or heard that's in your mind, although you may not remember it. It's for this reason, I think, that many of the readings have a biblical sound with the "thees" and the "thous" scattered throughout. Dad read the Bible through once for every year of his life.

A second source of psychic information is telepathy — a communication between one mind and another. If you could get into a person's subconscious mind like Dad could, you could give a beautiful diagnosis of his or her physical body. That would be the second source.

The third source is clairvoyance — the capability of somehow "seeing" things at a distance. Now whether he saw things at a distance the same way you and I might if we were there, I don't know. Not in every reading, but in a number of readings, he would make a side comment like: "What a beautiful cherry tree in the yard!" or "This man's arguing with his wife," or "There's been a wreck outside," and so forth. We always tried to check up on these comments, writing or calling and asking, "Do you have a cherry tree in your yard?" or "Were you arguing with your wife?" or "Do you have a beautiful Collie dog?" or something like that. He was never wrong. I never heard of a case when he was wrong.

On one occasion, I was listening to a reading that was given for a man in New York. This man was supposed to be in his apartment at the time of the reading. My mother, Gertrude, gave my father the suggestion, "You will have before you, the body of so-and-so, who is at this

address in New York ... " Dad lay there for a minute or
two and then said, "He's not here. He's on a bus coming
across town. There's been an accident and there's a lot
of traffic; the bus is late. He'll be here in minute. We'll
wait." He lay there for about 10 or 15 minutes and didn't
say a word. Then all of a sudden he said, "He's come in
now," and Dad proceeded to give the reading.

Well, when my Dad said that, Hugh Lynn got up
and went in the other room and called the man on the
phone. The man said, "That's exactly right. I know I was
supposed to be in my apartment at the time. I was on the
way and there was a traffic accident. The bus was late. I
just walked in." So there's something nobody could've
anticipated. I think his clairvoyance is pretty accurate.

The fourth place of getting information would be,
well there's two ways of looking at it. A lot of people
think there's such a thing as the Akashic Records—a
record of everything that ever happened in time and
space—and it's kind of like a big library. If you could
have access to that, you could have access to any kind
of information. Another way of looking at this fourth
source is to think about moving in another dimension,
like where you take a point, you move it, you have a
line—one dimensional—no height or depth in it. You
move the line at right angles to itself and you got a plane
—two-dimensions, no height or depth. If you move the
plane at right angles to itself, you would have a cube—
three-dimensions. That's the kind of world we live in.

Well, suppose you could move that cube at right
angles to itself. Well, how would you do that? We can't
conceive of moving that, but supposed you moved it in
time so it existed yesterday, today, and tomorrow. As
an analogy, think of a little two-dimensional bug that's
crawling in this plane and he has free will and he has
a memory. He remembers where he's been. He knows

where he is, but he knows nothing about what's going on up here or where he's going. But you're a three-dimensional person; you're looking down on this plane. You can see that bug, and you can see every place he's been. You can see where he is. You can see everything that could possibly happen to him in the future, and you can see it all at once—past, present, and future. Well, now you could say, if you continue to go like you're going, at three o'clock tomorrow you'll be right here, and you'd be right. But since he has a free will, he might choose to move in another direction. He might go this way or that way, and you'd be wrong. So that's why I don't think the future is fixed. I think that Dad could see future possibilities, some more likely than others.

In addition to these four sources, I think it's important to keep in mind that the attitudes and the purposes and ideals of the people involved in the readings affected his accuracy. I know for a fact that if Dad had a stomachache, or a cold, or was upset physically, he didn't get as good a reading as he did when he was perfectly healthy. On the other hand, if a mother had a sick child that she wanted to get well, Dad certainly wanted to help the child. This empathy between them, coupled with good intentions, good purposes, would result in a good reading. But if somebody was looking for a goldmine or buried treasure, what's the intention or motive? Dad felt he ought to help people. I don't know whether finding a goldmine would help them—might or might not. All kinds of things went into giving a reading.

I think Dad would be very surprised about how his work has spread all over the world, but I think he would be very happy about it. His hope was to help people as much as he could. He was most interested in helping people. If a person couldn't afford a reading, he'd give it to them for free. He was constantly giving to others.

While he was still alive and Tom Sugrue's book *There Is a River* came out, and the *Coronet* magazine article "Miracle Man of Virginia Beach" by Marguerite Harmon Bro came out at about the same time, he became famous overnight. At the time, Hugh Lynn was in Europe, and I was overseas, and neither of us could do anything to slow him down. The readings just started piling up. The bags of mail they brought in just buried him. He'd get so many calls at night; he even had to get an unlisted number. People called him up at midnight: "My mother's dying," or "My wife's dying, what can you do?" He was just deluged with people trying to get help.

Although the readings themselves recommended giving no more than two readings a day, he started giving 3, 4, 5, 6, 8, 10 readings a day just to try to help. It was too much, and he had a breakdown from it. He had a minor stroke, and he gave a reading on himself, and it told him he was trying to do too much; if he didn't slow down, it would kill him. He didn't slow down, and it killed him. That's what's happened.

When I think about it, Dad was happiest when the hospital opened and it was treating all these people. I guess that was his peak. That's what he had wanted most of all. And when the hospital folded, it was really a big disappointment.

I remember so many times watching my Dad on the fishing pier just thinking and fishing. He loved to fish. He loved to tend to his garden. He never came in from the garden without an armful of vegetables. He never came in from fishing without a load of fish. He was good at both of these things, but he loved helping people.

I think he'd be happy with how many people have been helped by the readings. If Dad were alive today, I think he'd be surprised by all of the books, by the readings on computer, and by the Edgar Cayce Centers around the world. Other than being surprised, I guess he'd still be giving readings as much as he could, and probably run into the same problems—wanting to help more people than he could. Dad would be surprised at how the organization has grown. He would be surprised at buying the old Cayce hospital building back and then at the size of the Library and Conference Center. He used to have a little library of books and now the A.R.E. has more than 70,000 volumes. I think he'd be surprised.

One of the readings that continues to stand out for me is something Dad said toward the end of a life reading. I think it shows Dad's focus on what is truly important. When an individual asked the question, "Who will aid me most in my work and daily life?" Dad's answer was short and to the point, "God!"—one word.

## Chapter Seven
# HAROLD J. REILLY

*Harold J. Reilly, PhT (1895-1987) was a prominent physiotherapist who owned and operated the Reilly Institute at the Rockefeller Center in New York City for more than 30 years. Among his patients were Bob Hope and Nelson Rockefeller.* He had five doctoral degrees, published many articles, was a noted lecturer, and was the author of the classic, The Edgar Cayce Handbook for Health through Drugless Therapy.

*The Cayce readings began referring individuals to Dr. Reilly even before Edgar Cayce had any conscious knowledge of Reilly or his work. Dr. Reilly began receiving case referrals from Edgar Cayce for about two years before they finally met. Eventually, the two became friends.*

*This information is a compilation of talks Dr. Reilly gave in 1975 and 1985.*

Edgar Cayce started sending people to me in 1930. At the time, I was running a health institution at Broadway and 63rd Street. The first person came in January, and he came in with what he called a "reading." Well, I had never heard of Cayce but I had treated and knew a lot of astrologers and psychics and all that, so I accepted it. Besides that, in those days I was building up a practice, and people were sending clients to me and I thought maybe Cayce was one of that group. I was used to getting patients who came to me for a special type of therapy, and I didn't pay too much attention to it. But these people kept coming in and naturally I got very curious both due to the way the readings were given — the special instructions in it, which challenged even some of my knowledge — and also the fact that I was building up a practice, and I thought well here's a man I better get to know.

I could understand the dictates of the readings because I had been in the field for twelve years, before ever hearing of Edgar Cayce. After getting clients referred to me for about two years, I got more interested. I thought, this man Cayce must be a genius or he must be in touch with something that we don't know about. He recommended things that even with all of my background and knowledge, I could not equal much less surpass. It gave me a lot of ideas and helped me with some of my cases. I decided it was about time that I met Cayce.

I got in communication with Edgar Cayce and asked when he was coming to New York again. So when he came up I met him, and we went out to lunch. Of course, I like to observe what people eat, and I thought, well, you certainly don't take readings on your diet. I asked him about it, and he said no. He said that if he got sick he would take a reading on himself to tell him what to do, but like all human beings, he was waiting until he got sick. I suppose because that is what we generally do. We don't do these things ahead of time, we wait until it hits us.

From then on, I got to know him quite well. I got to know him personally as well as through the readings, because I think he probably sent me more than 1,000 people over the fifteen years that I knew him. He would send people in for a massage and manipulation. Of course, that was my specialty. All my professional career, I specialized in exercise, massage, and manipulation. He'd send some in for exercise. In fact, out of the eight or nine thousand readings that were given for physical conditions, 1,300 were given for exercise, along with massage and hydrotherapy. Usually it was a combination of therapies, all of which worked into what I termed afterwards as "C.A.R.E." — Circulation, Assimilation, Relaxation, and Elimination. Believe me, when you get those things going in the body, the body doesn't have too much chance to be a breeding ground for germs. And if you keep the body in condition, you can repel a lot of these negatives — health negatives — because they give a fancy name to a sickness, and they become expensive that way. You just need a good colonic. You need a good massage. You need some exercise.

The great healing force in the body is circulation. Cayce stresses it. Don't forget two-thirds of all his readings have to do with health maintenance and the attainment of health. At least half of those have to do with some type of manipulation and massage. If you can't afford the luxury of a massage, the next best approach is exercise. It is something you can do for yourself. The trouble with exercise is that it doesn't cost you anything. That's one of the handicaps of exercise. How can it be helpful if it doesn't cost anything? Don't question it. Exercise and eating the right kind of foods might take some effort, but they're not going to cost you much money.

A lot of these health approaches are not too expensive, but some people would rather have a doctor give them some medication, or stick a knife in them, and end up giving them an expensive bill. So often, we get sick because of a lack of discipline — it's an accumulation of a lack of discipline that leads to some of these conditions. You might have a hereditary disposition toward certain things, but you can overcome that. You can overcome them. It takes discipline. You'll find that discipline in the Cayce readings.

Of course, if there are any serious complications or conditions, we like to have a doctor's checkup just to make sure there are no contraindications. I mean, you wouldn't give a man exercise who had very high blood pressure or a severe cardiac condition. Even now, they give mild exercise to those patients, but we used to avoid them altogether until they did some research.

Cayce would refer the individual and some of them were vascular cardiacs, but we went at them very easy and sort of built them up. Where they carried out the discipline, we never had any failures. I think the advice in the Cayce readings is the greatest thing we've had for 2,000 years.

When he sent a reading, I followed it — really followed it — because even though I had a lot of training in the things he had sent, sometimes there would be certain special instructions for the individual. Other times, he would just send it to me, "Take care of so and so, he has so and so," and leave it to my judgment. Sometimes he would tell me exactly what to do and what to give them, and invariably, when I followed his instructions, we had success. We had success in a lot of difficult situations.

My feeling after working with the information for forty-five years is I don't think there is anything in any field of healing that can surpass the instructions Cayce gave, because he didn't given them to cure symptoms, he gave them to cure the basis of the illness, not how it manifests itself. You get a cold. Why do you get a cold? Because you're full of toxins.

I found out several years ago that the National Casket Company does its biggest retail business in January. What happens is that during the summer you are out in the sunshine. You're exercising. You're swimming, and then you come indoors. Your mucus membranes dry out. Then Thanksgiving comes along and you load up on food—all kinds of food. Then you go onto Christmas; you are loaded with more. Then New Year's—the big celebration. By that time, you are a perfect culture medium for any good, active germ. So we get the cold season in January. That's why we suggest if you want to avoid colds, detoxify yourself. You do that with eliminations, either with sweat baths and colonics, or enemas, but keep your bowels normal and keep them working. You could also do that with food that has enough roughage, enough fiber.

Cayce draws attention to the emotional factors of diet, as well. In the book, *The Edgar Cayce Handbook for Health through Drugless Therapy*, I make the suggestion to take some of the Cayce philosophies and make them practical. For instance, we tell people if they have an upset stomach, or if they have a tendency to gastritis or a tendency to ulceration, eat slowly, and before you eat, sing for ten minutes. Because by singing for ten minutes you vibrate the gastric juices; you vibrate the muscles of the stomach itself, and then also, if you sing for ten minutes, you can't harbor negative thoughts— you might, but you'd have to try awfully hard. So you go to the meal feeling good.

I gathered these things from the Cayce readings. Other things I gathered, as well. For instance, Cayce gave an exercise called the cat walk. Now from that cat walk, I developed a series of seven exercises. That's how I worked with the readings and with the Cayce concepts. You know how they start in a race? The

runners get down on their hands and feet and go back
and forth? Well, I just do that exercise by going back and
forth without running.

The basic concepts — the philosophy you might say, as
I gathered from going through thousands of readings —
is that the basis of health is natural, spiritual, mental, and
physical. For instance, to put it more concrete, the same
blood that goes through your feet and your intestines
goes through your brain. You can affect your intestines
by how you think, but you can also affect your thinking.
You have toxic blood? Then you are going to think toxic.
You have a shock, then it will interfere with your bowel
action. Cayce had brought all that out long before we
had this wave of psychosomatic stuff. As far as I'm
concerned, psychosomatic starts in the intestines and
then affects the brain, but then, of course, the brain starts
to influence the body, and you get all these symptoms.

Cayce gave readings for individuals. For instance,
in arthritis you have to take about maybe ten or twelve
different types of approaches because, if you have
arthritis, it might be a little different than mine. Your
arthritis might have been caused by exposure, a trauma,
or a combination of both. Mine might have been caused
by emotional pressure. As far as the Cayce readings are
concerned, there are many approaches to arthritis. We
have found from our experience that you can contain
arthritis, but you can't say you are cured of arthritis,
because if you go back to living the same way you did
before, with weaknesses that might be hereditary or
acquired, you will develop the same kind of symptoms.

Cayce's medical terminology was always accurate.
He also drew attention to many things in both anatomy
and physiology and diet, which they are just finding
out about. We have attended seminars at Columbia,
and we had one at MIT on nutrition, and they were

saying some of the things Cayce talked about in the 1930s and 1940s. It was a new discovery for them. New approaches. You'd like to live 1,000 years just so you could keep working with the Cayce readings, seeing more of the things unfold. Sometimes it was a little subtle, because the terminology didn't conform to the terminology of the day, but now it's like Einstein with his theory of relativity. He had evolved the theory a long time before they proved it in practical matters. Cayce, I think, had access to some form of universal knowledge, because some of the things that Cayce recommended are found in the work of ancient physicians in Rome and Greece—things that they recommended.

Eventually, I had the opportunity to get to know Cayce a little better for myself, and have a reading. I had opened up a farm of about one hundred acres in New Jersey—about 38 miles from where I was in New York. Cayce, Hugh Lynn, and Gladys came to my place in New Jersey. They came up as my guests. I remember Edgar Cayce being pretty tired. The readings tired him out. Very few people realize that they tired him out physically and emotionally. One day, I thought, I'll let him rest, and I'll wait another day and then I'll try to get myself a life reading, because I had heard about his life readings and how fabulous they were.

It was quite a long reading. He was in a trance for fifty to fifty-five minutes. Besides the general life reading, I threw in a lot of questions about things that were troubling me at that time because it was the height of the Depression. I had been angling for a place in the Rockefeller Center, which was being built, but I didn't have enough money. They had given me a proposition where I was supposed to spend $150,000, which was like spending over $1 million today. That was a tremendous amount of money. Even with the

help from all my friends getting together, I had about
$8,000 to work with.

In the life reading, Cayce had told me about my
weaknesses and my strengths and all that, at the end
of the reading I asked a question. I asked him whether
I should continue my efforts negotiating with the
Rockefeller Center, because I had been working on it for
two and a half years, and believe me I was ready to give
up.

Question: "Is it advisable to continue my efforts to
secure an establishment in Radio City?"

Answer: "Advisable to continue. As we find, as
we have indicated, this should culminate in the latter
portion of the coming year, when those influences from
the efforts of others from without are attracted to the
activities of the entity, and bring better relationships."

Question: "Is there any special connections or
approaches that you would advise me to take in regards
to this?"

Answer: "The regular line of activities, the regular line
of association as we find during these periods necessary
for making the proper associations and connection,
will bring these to whom and how the activities will be
brought about for making the proper connections."

I felt the reading was quite encouraging after the
year of doubt and seeming impossibility of getting set
up in the Rockefeller Center. In fact, it gave me almost
too much confidence as you will see later in this story.
I decided to pursue this idea that the reading had
mentioned of working with the "efforts of others from
without."

At the time of the reading, I had been working with a
man in his forties for a couple of years, taking care of a
very serious problem. He had a kinked colon. He used
to go into a coma about every six months because of it.

His family, by the way, were the founders who financed the Lebanon Hospital in the Bronx. I had been able to resolve his going into comas. And so, I went to him and told him about my financial problem. I was fortified and encouraged by the reading I had gotten from Cayce. I laid it down for him because he was a builder. They had built a lot of houses in New York. After hearing my plans, he said to me, "I'll tell you what I'll do. I'll give you an $80,000 line of credit."

At the same time I had been working with this builder, I had been treating a couple of executives from RCA. One of them was Count Almonte, who was the evening manager of RCA broadcasting. I also had a patient who was an engineer on RCA's board of Directors. I had been working on him for quite some time, and had been able to give him a lot of relief, a lot of help.

When these two from RCA heard that the Lebanon hospital family was okaying my line of credit, they wanted to do business with me, as well. I soon had the money I needed to move forward on the lease — it would take me about eight years to pay all that off, but I had it. Sure enough, remember, Cayce had said it would be the latter portion of the next year, and fourteen months after the reading, in December 1934, the lease was sent to me for signature with everything I had been working for incorporated in it.

Now comes the even greater test and a characteristically human trait in me. During the negotiations and plans for my establishment, I found that my needs for space were even greater. I needed another thousand square feet of space. Would I try to change the terms of the lease or let well enough alone? Well, with the confidence generated by the Cayce reading, I took the long chance — I asked for an extra thousand feet at no extra charge. The Rockefellers okayed my request, and I got the extra thousand feet. I was happy, and Cayce was right. I had a very successful Institute in Rockefeller Center. We had the 8th floor in the RCA building on the 6th Avenue side from 49th to 50th Street. We had a crew of ten people just doing massage—five men and five women.

I sometimes liken the readings with a goldmine. The Edgar Cayce Foundation is sitting on a goldmine. We've picked up a few nuggets here and there, and we think that that's all the gold there is in the mine. I think we haven't hit the main vein yet. We are working towards it, and I think we are starting to pick up bigger nuggets—I feel I've picked up a few big nuggets myself—but I still think there is a great vein here we haven't even touched yet.

## Chapter Eight
## MAE GIMBERT ST. CLAIR

*Mae Gimbert St. Clair (1908-2003) was a native of Virginia Beach, but did not connect with Edgar Cayce until 1938 when she got a health reading for a serious problem. The reading helped her avoid surgery, and she became an intrinsic part of the "Work," which was to become her own life's work for more than sixty years – as a member of the office staff, receptionist, originator, and director of the Readings Research Department, compiler of readings by topic, lecturer, volunteer, and as a member of the Board of Trustees.*

*In her own life, she fastidiously followed the advice in the readings regarding health, continued a regular exercise program at a local gym, and maintained robust health and a hearty sense of humor well into her nineties. Her door was always open to those needing help or advice.*

*This information is adapted from two talks Mae gave at conferences – one in 1979 and the other in 1995.*

Suppose I tell you just a little bit about myself for starters? I was born three miles from the A.R.E. as the crow flies, in Oceana, on a farm, with a family of ten, and with the school just three blocks away. We'd walk to school and ride to church in a surrey with us young'uns hanging on here and there. Yes, I have been

here a long time, since the first of the century. There were
so many things here then that are not here now, such as
the sand hills with wildflowers and wild grapes. This
was the place that I grew up in.

It was to this place that Edgar Cayce chose to come
and spend a good part of his life—the part that fits me
in, anyway. He and his family came here in the 1920s,
wondering all the time. "Why here?" It was one of
the places that had been suggested in a reading. I am
very grateful that they came here, and that I eventually
connected with them.

How did it happen that I got connected with him?
Well, one day, I was walking along Pacific Avenue, and
I stopped to get a hamburger at this little shack that was
run by this handsome young man named Boyd Davis.
I didn't know it at the time but he was the brother of
Gladys Davis. We got to talking and he said, "Mae,
Edgar Cayce is lecturing at this hospital. He is lecturing
about reincarnation. Why don't you go up and listen to
the lecture?"

I hadn't heard the word but maybe one time when I
wondered if it had anything to do with transmigration.
I knew that I didn't want to be involved in anything of
the kind, and so I didn't do anything about it. My life
unfolded in another direction. I went to Florida to what
they call "hot curbs." That's where you drive up in your
car and give your order. That was quite an education in
itself! I will just mention in passing that I met someone
down there who knew about Edgar Cayce, of all things,
so this came into the picture once again without my
doing anything about it.

I came back home, wondering what I would do next.
I had been married and divorced in four and a half
years. I had not been a good student. I daydreamed my
way all through school. I couldn't pass algebra; made

a hundred in geometry. Nothing made any sense! So sooner or later it was destined, I guess, that I would know about Edgar Cayce.

I had gotten married and divorced in Virginia Beach, and after my divorce, I wanted to get away from my ex-husband, so I went to New York City where my sister was going to college at Columbia, trying to get her education in physical education and get her master's degree. I went up there just to get away from the scene of the crime, which was here. While I was up there, my aunt, who knew a few businesspeople in New York City, made a connection where I got a job working in a restaurant that didn't require any experience waiting on tables.

Well, that was very interesting and the most interesting part about this for me was that the second year I was there, two men came in and sat down, and I waited on them. One of the men noticed from my accent that I wasn't a New Yorker, so he asked me, "Where are you from?"

I told him, "Virginia Beach."

He said, "Do you know Edgar Cayce?" Well, of course I had heard of him, so he wrote a little note, and said, "Take this to Edgar Cayce, and he'll tell you what to do with your life." That man was David Kahn.

Well, I didn't believe in fortune telling, but this sounded different. So I brought the note home with me. I showed it to my mom. My mother, who had the greatest of wisdom, did not try to persuade me to do anything. Didn't even try to persuade me not to go down and talk to this man. Anyhow, I felt compelled to go down, so I did.

I can picture Edgar Cayce at the door of his home on 14th Street, across from the Catholic Church, opening the door, standing there he looked so tall, just tremendously

tall to me. Here I am down two or three steps, and I
handed him the note. He stepped back, invited me into
the hallway and into the living room. He handed me a
little pamphlet called "A Man and His Work," and sort
of gave me an opportunity to leave, which I took. No
more discussion at all. When I went home and told my
mom about this, she was even more puzzled, you know,
what is this strange thing all about? Having the greatest
of wisdom, she made no comments of any kind, just let
it hang where it was to see what would happen.

So time marched on. I wound up meeting someone
in New York City. I though that this person would
make a good husband. He's tall. He's presentable. He's
intelligent. I thought, I will never feel the way I felt in
the first marriage. Anyway, he came to Virginia Beach.
We got married. It didn't work out too well because he
was really a New Yorker, a Yankee, and I was really a
Southerner. At the time, those two did not meld well,
did not go together. The truth of the matter is he didn't
trust me, and I didn't blame him. I didn't blame him
because he didn't have any idea what was going on
in my thoughts. We struggled along for quite a while.
He finally got a job working nights, which was most
unfortunate because even when I went to the beach in
the daytime, I had to report where I had been and who
I had been with, which is totally foreign to my makeup.

One night, he dropped me off at a friend's house,
and a couple that I had not seen for a while came in to
visit this neighbor. This was the young man and his
wife, from whom I had bought the hamburger and had
asked me about the Cayce lecture. Later, I explained
some of the things that had been going on, and the fact
that I wasn't feeling well. Boyd said to me, "Why don't
you try Edgar Cayce?" He went on to explain that they
had a child who had been saved by Edgar Cayce. He

said that I should go and see if he could help me.

"How much does it cost?"

He said it was $20.

I said, "Don't 't have it."

He said, "Go and ask him. He will give you the reading regardless of money."

I thought, well, what have I got to lose?

So, I went to Edgar Cayce in January 1938. I was ill—I was very ill. I had had one tubular pregnancy, which resulted in the removal of one of my tubes. With the exception of my husband, I had not told anybody. I was experiencing the same symptoms, and I was terrified that I would have to have another operation. I got an appointment for a reading. I went in for the appointment, and I remember sitting there while he was giving the reading hearing words that I didn't even know what they were. The "thous" and the "thees" I had heard in church. I had never had an experience like this before. I thought, "What is going on here?"

All at once, asleep on the couch, Mr. Cayce started talking about "disturbances in the pelvic organs." He went on to say, "In the present there is the false conception. This has produced in the tube that is left (there's one) that of congestion." When I heard that, that did it! I hadn't told anyone about my current condition. He went on to say that an operation could be avoided if I followed the suggestions in the reading. More surgery had been my greatest fear.

When the reading was over, I went to the stairway at the front hall where they had a phone, and I called my mom and just told her, "Everything's going to be fine." Going from that to often staying with this couple, to having Gladys help me carry out the instructions that had been given and so forth; I got well.

I went down frequently just to talk to Mr. Cayce. He had this special chair in the southeast corner of the living room, and a large room with a fireplace on the west wall. I went to see him just to talk to him about everyday things. If this is so, how is that so? How does this work? And then, one day, I said to him, "Mr. Cayce, is there anything to this business of reincarnation?" And he gave me an affirmative answer. I wish I could remember his exact quote—I can't—but it was affirmative. I turned and said, "Oh, I'm meeting myself." Now, where did that come from? I had never heard it before. That was the beginning of my becoming more and more involved with the readings.

First, I had physical readings. I followed them; they worked. To be sure, my family thought I had flipped. But when they saw that I was sort of straightening up and beginning to put my shoulders back and face life again in a proper fashion, they got curious. Some of them got readings for themselves.

Having the physical readings, and applying them and being in the Cayce home a great deal because I was full of questions, I had many opportunities to just sit and talk with Edgar Cayce and get him to answer my questions one-on-one. Eventually, he began to ask me, "When are you going to get your life reading, Mae?" And I said, "When I can pay you what I owe you." I was paying him at the rate of $1 a month, just to show my good will.

Finally, he did an unusual thing. Mrs. Cayce told me he never does this sort of thing. He said, "Mae, you be here such and such a morning. We're going to get your life reading." Well, I was very excited. I reasoned that since the reading he had given me to correct my physical problem worked, there must be some validity to reincarnation. I began to get really excited about it.

Before we went in for the reading that day, he turned to me and said, "Mae, I can tell you that you will find out when you get your life reading that we were associated" and he said where. It just took my breath away. How could he do that?

We went in, and I expected to be immediately enlightened, of course. I sat down quietly with Gladys and Mrs. Cayce—Gladys with her pencil and pad, and Mrs. Cayce over by Mr. Cayce, as usual. She gave the suggestion that is given for life readings, and then Mr. Cayce began to count back from the present day to my time of birth and made some comments about much confusion. He finally got to the point where he said, "This doesn't mean that the entity will always be confused," which was a great relief to me.

He talked about the "entity." I had never heard that word before. And then he went into some things I didn't understand, at all. Confusion about the emotional influences and the astrological influences, and one thing after another. And then he went into, "Before this the entity was in the land of . . ." and proceeded to describe five or six incarnations that were influencing the present. The whole time, Mrs. Cayce and Gladys looked at each other with these all-knowing glances, and they were commenting with, "tch, tch, tch, tch," and so forth. I was just dying of curiosity, you know, to find out what all this meant.

I understood some of the things he said like, "When the entity weeps oft, she weeps alone." Some other things that were equally touching brought tears to my eyes. That anybody would even understand that I had a problem! As far as I was concerned, I was the only person who had a problem. My world was so small then.

I waited for that reading to be typed up by Gladys. I rolled it like into a scroll, still on the foot of the steps as I left that day. As I stood on the steps of that home, I knew I would not have traded those six typed pages for a million dollars. I knew that somewhere in this record, I was going to find the answers to what it is that I needed to know. I knew I was going to find the answers to where I came from, how I got here, and where I was potentially going.

I came to Mr. Cayce, handed him the reading, and asked him to explain things to me. He didn't take you into a long explanation about anything. You asked him a question; you got an answer. It was an interesting experience to be in the home with him and Mrs. Cayce. She is seldom mentioned, and she was so much a part of this whole scene — her lovely, quiet manner; her strength. She had fantastic strength. She handled things quietly, but you knew she was in command. She followed the readings where diet was concerned for her family. She was a marvelous balance for Edgar Cayce who was so given to going to extremes.

One day, he said to me, "Mae, go into the readings" — fourteen file cabinets of material at the time — "and copy everything that you can find on the time of the Master in the earth." This was for a lady who had a life reading and was told that she had been the first to hold the baby Jesus. She wanted to know everything, everything from the readings about that period of time. And that was my entry into the files and readings of Edgar Cayce. At the time I thought he was king bee. I didn't pay any attention to the fact that Gladys didn't seem to be upset about me going into the files. After all, this was her life's work. Everything was so peaceful and so calm in that house.

At the time, the readings were in these file drawers alphabetically arranged. I started out at the file drawer, the "A" drawer. I began to look for anything I could recognize as being from that period of time and copied it. I learned how to type doing this. You can imagine this was some project because my typing was not an expert job in any case! I spent whatever number of months it took to copy this material. Of course, the lady got her copy, but I had been exposed to the readings for the first time. Incredible privilege! Beyond description! That was the beginning of becoming acquainted with Edgar Cayce, the family, and the readings in one fell swoop, and the wonderment of so much new that I didn't know.

For some in my family unit, my advent into the Cayce home had caused quite a stir. It finally became very controversial, what I had gotten myself into, but my mother and father were very tolerant. They were so pleased to see me smile again. They were also kind of fascinated. I don't know that they ever understood it. It became possible for me, after Mr. Cayce passed to make up for some of the heartache I had caused them. Had it not been for Mr. Cayce, their lives would have been cut short because Mother and Dad both had problems and received physical readings. The things that we were told to follow worked and extended their lives at least twenty years.

I knew the Cayce people—I knew the family. I learned how to be helpful to them. Whatever I am today is a result of being in that wonderful environment— the tremendous love that they exuded. The caring, the laughter, the humor, the stumbling, and all of the things that took place. I felt totally free. I was not perfect, and I knew that I wasn't, but it didn't matter. I was always welcome. I was able to be with the Cayces through some of the difficult times. I couldn't help them enough. I was there when the mail came in by the boxful, and when Mr. Cayce was no longer giving readings. I was there with him when he died.

We look on the outside of things; Mr. Cayce looked on the inside. He looked at the heart of the matter. He emphasized and magnified the virtues, minimized the faults. He encouraged people to reach for agreements — forget the differences. Pray together. Play together. And grow together. Then we can think of life as being a little bit different than, "How can I get out of here and not have to come back?" People will say, "How many incarnations do I have to have?" As long as we feel that way about it, we have a ways to go. We are not willing to learn our lessons, apparently, when we begin to entertain that kind of thought.

As for the readings, I handled them as if they were my very own. They are what I am today; I hope. That exposure, and that love, and that great moment in time — sometimes it feels like just a moment in time. What a privilege!

I'd like to close with my favorite Cayce reading affirmation, which goes something like this, "Let the heaven of the consciousness of the presence of the Christ light your pathway of choice, that you may choose in this life to be that for which you were created."

## Chaper Nine
## LYDIA J. SCHRADER GRAY

> *Lydia J. Schrader Gray (1889-1982) obtained a*
> *number of readings from Edgar Cayce for health,*
> *personal guidance, and on the topic of reincarnation.*
> *A widow and former concert singer, for twenty-five*
> *years she dedicated her life to furthering Cayce's work*
> *and served as a lecturer, numerologist, hostess, and*
> *"house mother" for A.R.E.'s headquarters building—*
> *the former Edgar Cayce hospital.*
>
> *This is adapted from a "Searchlight" article she*
> *wrote about her experiences with Mr. Cayce, as well*
> *as one of her lectures on Edgar Cayce's psychic ability.*

Some of you may have known Edgar Cayce personally; some of you may have friends who knew him and who have been helped by him, both physically and spiritually. Some of you became acquainted with him by reading his life story, *There Is a River* by Thomas Sugrue, and *Many Mansions* by Gina Cerminara. I'd like to share with you my first meeting with this developed soul.

I was living in New York at the time, attending a course of lectures on comparative religions. One evening when I was driving one of the other members of our class back to her hotel, I mentioned that I was puzzled by a swelling and a seeming fever in my left cheek, which occurred nightly but seemed to disappear each morning. I had been to my dentist but he found nothing wrong. He suggested that I go to a sinus specialist. She interrupted me and said, "You ought to have a Cayce reading." I replied, "Who's Cayce? I've never heard of him."

She said, "He is going to be in New York next Tuesday evening at the McAlpin Hotel. There is to be a lecture given by four doctors and a psychic. He is the psychic."

Well, I went to that meeting; there were about 500 people in attendance. I can assure you that it has meant more to me than any other lecture that I have ever attended, and I have listened to many, for I've been a student of metaphysical truths over a period of many years.

A certain David Kahn, who had had many readings and who knew Mr. Cayce for many years, opened the meeting. He told of how he had been led by the readings, step by step, from a position in a grocery store to a position of wealth and success in the radio cabinet business.

Next spoke Harold J. Reilly, a physiotherapist and head of the Reilly Health Service in New York City. He told of people arriving at his office in the 1930s with their Cayce readings, asking him if he could give them the treatments prescribed therein. The treatments suggested: therapy baths, colonics, and massage. This went on for two years before he ever met Mr. Cayce, and he wondered how and why he was chosen to administer these treatments.

Dr. Frank Dobbins, an osteopath, whose office was then on Fifth Avenue, told his amazing story. He had just come from Maine and established himself on Staten Island. His shingle was out, as he put it, but his name was not as yet in the telephone book. One afternoon a lady presented herself at his door, with her young daughter. She asked him if he would treat her daughter, as suggested by a reading, which she handed to him. He questioned her, and asked, "What sort of a reading?" and she hesitantly answered, "A reading from a psychic." He was flabbergasted. His first reaction was to refuse, then he thought of his doctor's oath—to aid all who come to him for help—and said, "If you will allow me to examine your daughter, I'll make my own diagnosis. Leave this reading with me and this evening I will study it. Come tomorrow, and I will tell you whether I can accept the case or not."

So, that evening he settled himself down in an easy chair, and began to read it. He had been brought up in Maine, where they are very conservative, and he had many misgivings. Chills, ran up and down his spine, as he read, "Yes, we have the body of . . ." The diagnosis of what was wrong was given and specific osteopathic treatments were suggested. He said that he nearly jumped out of his chair when he read this question: "To whom shall I go for my daughter's treatments?" and the answer given was, "Find Dobbins!!"

After Dr. Dobbins worked with the young girl, he found that he agreed wholeheartedly with the diagnosis and treatment; after that, Dr. Dobbins claimed that the readings had helped him in correctly diagnosing 95% of his cases.

Dr. Henry S. W. Hardwicke, an M.D., impressed me greatly when he said, "Every reading, whether a physical or a life reading, is a challenge to every soul who receives one." It is challenging—and those meeting this work for the first time will find this to be true.

Just before Mr. Cayce was to speak on this momentous evening David Kahn announced that a man had just entered the hall, whose story he wanted to tell, though it was really not scheduled to be on the program. This man had been ill for three years, going from one doctor to another, until he was finally put into a mental institution.

Mr. Kahn proceeded to tell us that years ago, when his children were young, he had a governess for them, and, just like everyone else in his household, she heard many marvelous stories about Mr. Cayce and his great gift. She had been gone from his employment for many years when she suddenly appeared at his office, asking him if that man Cayce was still alive and was he still giving readings? The gentleman who had been committed to the institution was her brother-in-law. She was so moved by her sister's desperation that she suddenly thought of her former employer and his great faith in Mr. Cayce.

A reading was given immediately. Mr. Kahn telephoned Virginia Beach and gave the name and address of the patient and the first sentence spoken was, "Yes, we have the body . . ." The reading went on to describe how this man was in an institution where he did not belong. The reading stated that he had fallen on the ice as he left the Grand Central Post Office three years earlier and had injured his spine. Osteopathic adjustments were suggested. Based on Cayce's advice, the man's relatives saw to it that the suggestions were administered and the patient became well and returned to normal.

It was a touching moment when the gentleman came to the front of the hall and in a quiet, choked voice said, "Every word Mr. Kahn has spoken is true, and I came tonight to shake the hand of the man who gave me back my life." He and Mr. Cayce shook hands, and I can assure you there was hardly a dry eye in the hall as the gentleman returned to his seat.

When at last Mr. Cayce arose, my friend, who knew him so well, whispered to me; "He won't talk much about himself, but he'll give us a good sermon. He'll preach at the drop of a hat."

Mr. Cayce, a tall, thin, quiet man, with a sensitive face and a charm hard to define said, "I feel like exhibit A. I know many of you have had readings and have been benefited, but I of myself have done nothing. I am but a channel for this great gift, and I feel that I am more helpful to you asleep than when I'm awake." Then he gave us one of the finest sermons I have ever been privileged to hear—reminding us that we are meeting "self" in whatever problem confronts us, telling us that we should let the motivating influence in us be the love of God, as it manifests itself in our actions towards our fellow man.

When the lecture was over, I went up to shake his hand, like so many of the others in the big ballroom. As soon as he took my hand, he turned to Hugh Lynn, and said, "Make an appointment for this lady for tomorrow."

Well, I can tell you I was there at 3:30 p.m. sharp. I knocked on his hotel room, and I remember he opened the door and looked down at me—he was very tall—and he asked, "Were you surprised when I said to schedule you for an appointment?" Well, I certainly was surprised and thrilled, and then he said, "I recognized you."

I said, "Mr. Cayce, I never saw you before last night."

He said, "When you have your reading, you'll understand."

Well, I had my reading; couldn't wait for it. I found out we had been together in Egypt—that's how he recognized me.

You know, he didn't have to be asleep for some of his psychic experiences. There is another occasion that stands out very clearly in my mind. It was the time when Hugh Lynn was going off to war. He was at the house with a couple of his buddies, and they were all getting ready to serve their country. Cayce looked at Hugh Lynn and took his son aside and said, "Hugh Lynn, your mother and me, we won't be here when you come back. You will come back but those two boys won't." They hadn't even gone to war yet, and somehow he knew.

After my life reading with Mr. Cayce, I arranged for a physical reading for myself and a life reading for my niece. We drove to Virginia Beach for these readings, but as you well know, a trip such as this was entirely unnecessary. The cause for the swelling in my cheek was given. It had nothing to do with my teeth or sinus but was caused by the lack of proper drainages and acidity of the blood. Suggestions were given to correct this condition and at the same time I was told to take "Codiron." Mr. Cayce told me an interesting story about this. The first time the use of this Codiron came through a reading, the lady for whom it was prescribed could not procure it. Her druggist never heard of it. She was given in her reading the name and address of a firm in Chicago and they in turn wrote asking her how she had heard of Codiron, for they had it but as yet had not even put it on the market!

I could go on and on, but if you read the books, *There Is a River* by Thomas Sugrue, and *Many Mansions* by Gina Cerminara, you will read case after case where, through his great gift, he restored to health and happiness many who came to him for aid. You will read of his own doubts and fears, of his determination to give up his business, which was photography, and devote his entire time to the giving of readings after his wife's life was spared, and Hugh Lynn's eyesight was restored, and his younger son healed. Then and only then did he say, "God, I don't understand, but for the good that has come to me, may I be able to help others when they ask." My reading suggested that I should come to Virginia Beach. When I asked what I should do the answer was simple, "Do with your hands what your hands find to do." When I came down, I didn't hardly get my nose inside the door when I was busy right off the bat—I've been busy ever since. After Mr. Cayce died and Mrs. Cayce passed away three months later, Gladys was busy in the office, and you can imagine how far things were behind after Cayce's illness. I helped Gladys write every thank you letter that she had. I could at least do that. She sat there in a chair and dictated, and I wrote letters and did everything I could do to help—stuff envelopes and all the business they had to do to send things out. Everyone was so busy that there was just no one to take care of the house. Everyone was gone. We were renting out rooms to two young sailors and their wives, so I started taking care of the house and really became the housekeeper.

I was trying to keep the house clean, looking after the sailors and their wives. When they were in the kitchen, there'd be crumbs all over the floor and the kitchen sink wasn't as clean as I wanted it. So, I'd go in there and clean up after them, but in my mind I was really resenting it. It is a good example of nothing happening by chance. One day after cleaning up, I went and studied some of the readings. I picked up a reading and came across this passage: "Unless there is joy in your heart for whatever task you are doing, you haven't gained one iota."

So I went downstairs to those kids. I can see myself standing in the doorway between the kitchen and the dining room. They were in the kitchen, and I said, "I gotta be joyous cleaning up after you kids." And you know what, not only did it change my attitude after that but the girls got a little better with the dustpan and the brush. Things got a little cleaner than they had been before.

There have been so many times that I've learned a lesson from the readings. The soul has to grow, you know. I had a brother named William. He didn't understand me. We hadn't spoken in ten years, and I had basically given him up. The readings talk about being honest, and loving, and kind, and forgiving, and then I started thinking about William. I had tried to be forgiving where William was concerned, or so I thought.

Now Mr. Cayce had told the first study group to get up at 2 a.m. and meditate. So I decided I was going to get up at 2 o'clock and just send out wonderful thoughts and the Christ Consciousness to William. I prayed that there would be love between us. I did it for about a month.

I knew from my niece, William's daughter, who I was still in touch with, that he had to travel by car from Massachusetts to Florida several times a year. All of a sudden, I got this urge to write William and tell him that I had heard from his daughter that he was going down to Florida, and I invited him to stop and see me here in Virginia Beach on his trip down. I got a letter from him that I never expected. My first thought was to wonder if the leopard had changed his spots. It was just wonderful. He told me he couldn't make it on the way down but he would stop on the way back up to Massachusetts.

Do you know he came to the headquarters building and came up those back stairs, and we met at the door, and kissed. Not one word was ever said about the past. The past was absolutely wiped out. I'm going to tell you it works. It works if you take the time. The past can be healed; it can be redone. We all have this capacity. We all have psychic ability.

I remember one day when I was visiting with Edgar Cayce, a young lady came to call. She was the picture of health, vibrant with joy. She had some x-ray pictures with her that she wanted him to see. After she left, he told me her story. She was given up to die by a number of physicians, as she had tuberculosis. When she heard of Edgar Cayce and his great powers, she sought out his help. Through the readings, she was restored to perfect health. Mr. Cayce said to me, "It's cases like this that make my life worthwhile. They help me to face the laughter and ridicule of those who are ignorant."

You have only to read his life story to know how cruelly he did suffer from ridicule and from intellectual arrogance. He was known as the world's greatest psychic—"the Miracle Man of Virginia Beach." We who knew him know that he did not consider his work miraculous but those who did not understand his psychic gift felt that he was performing miracles.

Many have asked, How did Mr. Cayce develop this gift? Many who might be interested speak of the psychic only behind closed doors. Why? Have any of you looked up the word psychic in the dictionary? Webster defines psychic thus: "Of or pertaining to the human soul, or to the living principle of man." Why should we hesitate to know more about our souls? For a psychic, or one who is clairvoyant, is a developed soul in evolutionary growth. He is one closely attuned with the infinite as were the prophets of old, as was Jesus, the most highly developed soul of all, and He came to show us the way. Edgar Cayce was such a developed soul. He came into this earth plane, in this incarnation, with his soul, his psychic senses fully developed—attuned to the infinite.

This question was given to Mr. Cayce as he slept. "Where did Edgar Cayce get his power?" The reading stated that he had developed a mental faculty which enabled him to withdraw from physical consciousness. This free mind quality, which he called the soul-mind, could be directed by suggestion to specific persons, times, and places. While this attunement existed, he could bring through word-descriptions of his impressions. These impressions were not limited to the three dimensions of the normal five senses but were drawn from what is sometimes known as the Akashic Records. The readings also indicated that in previous incarnations he had reached a point in growth of individual consciousness from which, impelled by the desire for service, he could act as an integrating clarifying agent for those who sought his guidance.

Each and every one of us has psychic forces or soul forces latent, within us. Whether we wish to develop them or not is an individual matter. We are here on this earth plane for spiritual unfoldment. We must consciously become aware of this fact, and then try to apply it in our daily lives.

"How can one know the infinite?" was asked by a seeking soul. The answer was that it is not by the act of thought or reason. The infinite is out of the realm of ordinary reasoning. We can only comprehend the infinite by a faculty that is superior to reason. That faculty is the psychic force or soul force. If we abuse our psychic faculties, or if we allow them to be ridiculed, then we build a barrier to prevent those faculties (latent within each individual) from developing toward the infinite. If we have the proper conception of what psychic means, then we know it is a faculty which exists, has existed and is ours by birthright, because we are sons and daughters of God. We have the ability to make association with the Spirit, for God is Spirit, and seeks such to worship Him.

Now that Mr. Cayce has passed on, what becomes of his work? Many had thought that the Association would close its doors, for during his lifetime individuals were involved for their personal readings. But the readings themselves named the association formed to study his work, the "Association for Research and Enlightenment." The readings often said that the work should be presented: first to the individual, then to the groups, then to the classes, and then to the masses. That is the association—the individuals who make up this work.

The research is concerned with the thousands of individual readings which he left and the significance of his unusual experiences. Its first aim is to provide you with the information that will help you where you are. The simple principle of giving to others what we find to be good is the foundation of our work. It might be termed an educational program to bring to people everywhere a better understanding of the soul, of our relationship to God, and of our relationship to one another.

The enlightenment flows from the use of this remarkable information in individual lives through practical help for the physical body, stimulating philosophy for the mind, and an understanding of universal laws for the soul. This work, therefore, is threefold, focusing on spirit, mind, and body functioning as one.

I believe I can truthfully say that from the moment I came in contact with Mr. Cayce, from that time forward, my life has been more purposeful.

## Chapter Ten
# ELSIE SECHRIST

*Elsie Sechrist (1909-1992) was trained as a registered nurse. She met Edgar Cayce in the early 1940s and began a long and continuing interest and involvement in the study of parapsychology. Internationally recognized as an authority on dreams and meditation, she and her husband, Bill, lectured all over the world, becoming A.R.E. international representatives, and inspiring volunteers to create Edgar Cayce groups around the world. She was also a lifelong advocate of A.R.E.'s Study Group program. Among her publications were two books which have become classics:* Meditation: Gateway to Light *and* Dreams Your Magic Mirror. *She appeared many times on various talk shows, including the* Mike Douglas Show, *as an authority on dreams.*

*This is adapted from interviews Elsie gave in 1975 and 1984.*

I hope I can share with you the excitement of one of the most important experiences of my life — this was my meeting with Edgar Cayce. My husband and I had both had readings while we were in New York, and this was shortly after the book, *There Is a River*, had been published. I then went down to Virginia Beach, not knowing really what to expect. The life reading had been very impressive in that he seemed to have pinpointed many important things that lay deep down in my own heart and mind, some of which I had never discussed with any living soul. It just didn't seem possible that he had been able to do this, and I had to go see for myself. I didn't know what to expect. I really didn't know what was going on down at this place called Virginia Beach so I went with almost fear, and trembling, and awe at the same time.

When I got to Virginia Beach to meet this man, I must confess that I was a bit disappointed. I expected to see somebody that looked very unusual, statuesque; with perhaps a shining countenance, and very handsome, but he looked like a country doctor. A simple person. You wouldn't turn around in the street if you saw him, but once you spoke to him, his voice was soft, it was direct, it was honest, it was embracing. For me, I always saw a double-pupil, as if he were looking through eternity. It made you a little uncomfortable, at times, because you wondered what you had done yesterday, or said yesterday, that you ought not to have. And yet, after you got to know him, you knew he wasn't anyone who ever condemned. If he ever told you anything about a negative side of your nature, he would do it in such a way that you considered it a blessing.

I was at a June conference. As I sat there listening to him talking, an inner voice said, "You have come home. You need seek no longer." And I knew that in some way this was going to be the answer. At that time, he was not as well-known as he became later, and there were perhaps forty people who were attending this conference. During the program, he asked those of us who would like help with meditation to raise our hand. I was among them. I raised my hand. He said, "All right, I will awaken you at 2 a.m. in the morning." I said, well, I don't have a telephone in my room. He said, "Well, I don't need a telephone."

My room was on the oceanfront several blocks away from the headquarters. We were then staying at the Essex House, which had no telephones and, of course, headquarters was at the old Cayce home down on 14th Street. I thought—I just met him—is this strange man going to come to my room at two in the morning? Then I thought, well, I have a friend staying with me so I guess it will be all right if he does come.

That night, I awakened exactly at two! I knew nothing about meditation except it had to do with God, and suddenly I saw one big blue eye staring at me. Well, what are you going to do with one eye—like looking through a keyhole? You just look, that's all. And then, that changed and the room was flooded with the odor of gardenias. Now I was on the oceanfront! There were no flowers around. I thought what have I gotten myself into? If it hadn't been for the fact that my roommate in the morning said, "Elsie, did you awaken during the night and smell gardenias?" I might have thought that this was my imagination.

Anyway, when I met him the next morning, I said, "Mr. Cayce, I had some experiences. Could you help me?"

He said, "Before you tell me about your experiences, let me tell you of the dream I had before I awakened you." He said, "I dreamed that I met with you in a garden and you asked me for help in meditation. I told you, you must meditate through the all-seeing eye, and you said, "Well, that is not enough! I also need the odor of gardenias."

This was the first experience that I had with this man.

This experience with being awakened for meditation during the conference continued. Every morning, I would awaken at 2 a.m. However, once I awoke at 2:20

in the morning, and I seemed to see Mr. Cayce's face laughing. The next morning I told him, "Oh, I am so sorry you couldn't awaken me."

He said, "You thought you had overslept, and in fact, I had overslept—that's why I was laughing."

He did this for me for many, many months after the conference, awakening me. And then one day I heard him say, "Well, I think it's enough now. You can do this on your own."

Of course, I did continue but changed my hour of meditation. Two in the morning is for the birds!

I felt such a connection with this man that I knew somewhere along the line, perhaps in other lifetimes, we had been associated. As I studied my readings, I realized that this was true. There were many times when my husband and I went to Virginia Beach to watch Edgar Cayce do his work. He would loosen his tie and his shoestrings. He would lay down, put his hands up to his forehead for a moment. When the person giving the suggestion could see that he seemingly had lost consciousness, the suggestion was given. And then in a very simple and normal way, he began to speak.

It was as if he were present with the individual for whom he was giving the reading. The individual might be thousands of miles away, and Cayce would comment about the lovely pajamas the person had on. Or he might talk about the room in which the person lived. One time, he mentioned an accident had taken place outside of the home of the woman for whom he was given the reading—she had not even become aware of it yet.

Perhaps the outstanding thing that I felt about this man was the great love that he had for others. This you felt immediately upon coming into his presence. I think it would be important to mention that people like to sanctify a person like that, make him a saint, put him up on a pedestal, but Edgar Cayce had especially physical weaknesses. We were out with him more than once having dinner, and he knew he wasn't supposed to eat highly seasoned food, and I remember one time we were with Mrs. Cayce, and she said, "Now Edgar, you shouldn't order that. You know it doesn't . . ." And he interrupted her and said, "I want it." And when he said it that way, there were no other words. We saw him the next day, and he was just green! He said, "My wife was right. I was up sick all night long." On other occasions she'd say, "Edgar, you're smoking too much." I remember one time after dinner, we were sitting out on the lawn and Mr. Cayce was lighting one cigarette from the butt of another. Mrs. Cayce said, "Edgar! Why are you smoking so much?" He said, "I don't have any more matches!"

None of us who knew Edgar Cayce will ever try to make him a saint because he was not. He was a human being who had, according to the readings, worked at being of service to others down through the ages. He was as easily able to give a reading for someone in America as he was to someone in Europe, or any other part of the world.

Some of you may have heard about the reason why he refused to play cards, because if you held up a whole deck of cards, he could tell you every card that you held in your hand, and he was too honorable to take advantage of anyone. I remember another story that had to do with his meeting a woman one day in a restaurant. He could see from her aura that something tragic might happen in her life, and he stopped her—a complete stranger—and said, "If I were you, I wouldn't get into an automobile for the next 24 hours." Well, you can imagine the woman eyes nearly popped out and her mouth fell open, but apparently she took it seriously.

The next morning, he was having breakfast in this hotel dining room and when the woman walked in, looked around the room, spied him, and came running over. She told him that she had planned to go in an automobile with her sister, taking a trip somewhere in the Blue Ridge Mountains. She had refrained from doing so because of what he had told her and her sister had gone over the cliff, and was badly injured.

In my own life reading, I remember he started my life reading by saying there had been changes as in 1932, and changes in 1939, and there definitely were big changes in those two years. How did he know that?

In my husband Bill's life reading, there were three points that he made that were simply outstanding; they showed the ability of this man to pick out of a personality deep-seated urges and motives within the individual. He said that my husband had abilities as a salesman that went back to a Persian incarnation when he had led a camel caravan. At the time, he had been a dealer in cloth. Something hit me between the eyes when he said that, because there were many times when I used to get so angry at Bill, because if I bought a dress and came home with it, the first thing he did was to take the material between his fingers and feel it. Most of the time he'd say, "It's cheap. It's cheap. I don't care what you paid for it."

I'd say, "What do you know about cloth?"

He also said that Bill had the ability to imitate the call of the birds, which came from an experience just before this when he associated with the Indians. So, I asked my husband, "Can you do this?" And he said, "Oh yes, I've been able to do it all my life." Well, I had been married to him for many years and had never seen him do it. There was a great big owl up on one of the trees, and I said, "Let me see what you can do."

And he did it. He called out to the owl and the owl responded back!

Cayce also said my husband had ability as an engineer, as he had served as an engineer in Rome when he was among the first to build bridges. I knew he was always interested in these kinds of things. He loves to design. This man, Edgar Cayce, had the most unusual ability. To be able to tell us things about ourselves when he didn't know us at all.

The important thing about the depth of this man, Edgar Cayce, was that as I read my life reading every year, I find new things in there that I didn't see before. In my own life reading, Cayce gave me about four past incarnations that were important in the present. I might say, and I am sure other people can verify this, that those who continue to work at prayer and meditation will have many other lifetimes revealed to them. I had at least twenty other lifetimes revealed to me after that. But the ones that he gave me were the most important and related to this particular lifetime. He gave me one in early America near Providence, Massachusetts when my name was apparently Elsie Gilchrist.

We went to Salem last year, and I really had a feeling of going home, I really felt very much at home. But even greater was my surprise when we saw that the whole town was named after the Gilchrists—the streets, the banks, the library buildings, and so on. I might have been a poor cousin, but the name of Gilchrist was very, very common over there. He said that during that time I was associated with the Indians and helped them a great deal.

The next incarnation that he gave me was in the Holy Land. He said that I was there on the day of Pentecost, and he mentioned, "those things of such natures still find a distant chord in the entity's consciousness." And he was exactly right! I remember when I went to Sunday School and church and whenever that story was told, I saw the disciples standing there, and I saw the split tongues of fire descending over their heads. There was still a distant cord of memory of that in my consciousness.

The next lifetime he gave me was the Persian incarnation. Bill and I hope to go back to Iran at some point, as we think we found the location of the place where Cayce had founded a center back then—near present day Shushtar.

In addition to Cayce's psychic talent, I think that perhaps another part of this man's nature that was so unusual was his great humility. It almost seemed as if he were deprecating his ability. I think the question that was asked or presented to Mr. Cayce more often than any other, "Mr. Cayce, you are so wonderful, how do you do all this?" His answer always was, "You can do this too." He said, all of us have the same source. We all are an externalization of God, the Creative Force, which makes it possible for all of us to do all the things that any human being ever did in the earth, including our guide, Jesus the Christ.

He said that within all of us there are also buried not only the talents, the experiences, the memories that we have had from the beginning of time but that divine self which is just waiting for us to be awakened. He said that perhaps the last remaining door for all of us that remains available even in our present state is the dream state. It is through the dream state, especially after meditation, that we open up the doors of all the levels of our own consciousness to all time and space. In this time and space lie, of course, the secrets of the universe, our own experiences, those talents that we have achieved and which we may pick up and bring to the surface when we begin to use them properly.

He said meditation was that which every single soul had to do. Prayer is talking to God but meditation is listening so that the Divine within may begin to speak to us personally. In my own experience, I have found nothing that is of greater help than meditation, because it does keep you awake to your own faults, it keeps that Creative Force flowing. You find that you have a great deal more energy to do the vital, important things.

For forty years, Bill and I have been in Study Group work and have had them in our home all those times. It has been one of the greatest blessings, greatest opportunities, not only in the opportunities that it gave us to see the change in people who came in with long faces, unhappy, not understanding life, and so on, and seeing them transformed, and seeing marriages cemented, and love relationships and families helped. Even learning to love your mother-in-law — because if you don't, she's going to come back and be your sister or your wife or something else! He pointed out that even your neighbors are going to come back lifetime after lifetime, so don't try to run away!

For me, what was so very, very important in these readings is that there is nothing unjust in life. Now you may think you get away with something, like a person who may have gotten away with murder in this life — but he'll pay for it in the next and wonder why he's unjustly accused. There is nothing that occurs in your life that isn't there by the permission of the Divine within yourself because you need that experience. And you can't complain, then. You can't ever complain because it is an experience you have drawn to yourself.

It's the Study Group Program that really encourages personal growth because every one of those chapters is in the development of the understanding of how you become a true child of God. God will speak to you in dreams and visions, and the still small voice. The voice of your conscious self will speak louder and more often. You become far more sensitive to the needs of others. You may sit next to somebody and know that she is desperate, because she has the need of some money, and if you've got it, you better just slip it to her. These are some of the things it behooves you to do when you become sensitive to other people and their needs. A kind word or something else, and you do become very sensitive to people and their needs. But also, you really, truly know that the Lord is your keeper. And what more could you want out of life?

I would like to close by sharing what my relationship with Mr. Cayce and his work has meant to me. It has been my whole life. It has put light and meaning upon everything that is important to a human being — marriage, religion, God, the Christ, friendship. There's nothing that puts that glow and that beauty and that love into your heart for all human beings when you have the understanding that Cayce gave us.

## Chapter Eleven
## EULA ALLEN

*Eula Allen (1899-1978) was a "Navy wife" who moved from coast to coast with her husband, Harold, before the couple finally settled in Norfolk, Virginia. She was referred to Edgar Cayce for a physical reading by a neighbor. Later, she obtained life readings for herself and readings for members of her family. She was a frequent participant in study group meetings, prayer group meetings, and Edgar Cayce's Tuesday night Bible class. After Edgar Cayce's death, she became very active in A.R.E. Headquarters activities.*

*Known for her compassion and her warmth, she became a popular speaker for A.R.E., especially on the topic of her books "The Creation Trilogy" (Before the Beginning, The River of Time, and You Are Forever).*

*This is a compilation of an interview she gave in the 1960s and one of her lectures in the 1970s.*

I would like to share with you what the readings and the work of Edgar Cayce has meant to me and my family. In my first marriage, I had three children. I didn't marry Harold until my children from the first marriage were grown. My youngest son was sixteen before I remarried. Eventually, all the children were gone and grown. Harold was in the Navy, and we had moved far away from everybody I knew. Here I was with no

children. All at once I began to get the feeling that there
was a soul that wanted to come in. I thought, "Well, yes,
I would like to have another child, and Harold wanted a
child." So I prayed about this. I was way up in my forties
by that time, so it took quite a while but I kept feeling
this somebody around me. Finally, we were able to have
a child. Unfortunately, Harold was shipped out, and so I
was all alone in the city of Norfolk.

I was very ill after Lorie, my youngest child was
born. In fact, I had been sick for years. Having the baby
made things worse. I got congestion of the kidney. The
left kidney had swollen to the size of a cantaloupe. I had
intense pain in my back. I often had a high temperature.
I had anemia. My general health was so depleted, I was
down to 108 pounds, which is very low for someone my
height. The doctor wanted to remove the kidney because
it was so swollen that it stuck out in the middle of my
back. I told him that I couldn't do it. I explained that I
have a baby and my husband is gone. I just can't do it.
So he made me sign a release that said the hospital had
done everything they could, and they didn't agree with
my decision.

My neighbor had heard that I wasn't well, and that
I had a baby and so she came to see me. I was renting
a room from a woman in Norfolk, and she was helping
me with the baby. The neighbor came in and talked with
me a little while, and I ended up telling her all of my
troubles. There was a Unity book laying on the side of
my bedtable, and she asked, "Do you study Unity?" I
told her I did. She said, "Well, I don't know how you're
going to take this but since you've studied Unity, maybe
it will be alright. I know someone that can cure you."

I had been through all kinds of doctors and hospitals
and what have you, and I said, "Well, who is this doctor?"

She said, "He isn't a doctor. I don't know what

you will think about this but he cured me. They said I had cancer of the stomach, and he said it was an accumulation of toxins and poisons in my system. I was cured."

I asked, "How did he know that if he isn't a doctor?"

She answered, "Well, his superconscious contacts yours, and it tells him what's the matter with your physical body, and what you can do about it."

I thought about that for a minute and asked, "When can I see this man?"

She said, "You don't have to see him. You can lie right here in the bed, and I'll go call him now and see if he can give you a reading."

So she went and called Mr. Cayce, and he told her that he would give me a reading in the morning. I didn't meet Edgar Cayce until after I had the reading.

The reading said that I had an infection of the kidney caused by a lack of blood and proper circulation to carry the waste and the infections away from the body. The reading went on to say there wasn't anything organically wrong with the organs of the body; it was mostly improper circulation. The digestive tract had lost its ability to take up and absorb food properly. The reading recommended a change in diet: no beef, no pork—instead only fish, lamb, and poultry. It recommended plenty of leafy vegetables and fruit. It recommended that we use an electrical vibrator up and down the spine for about a half hour before going to sleep. It also recommended vitamin D and vitamin B, taking olive oil every day for ten days. It recommended walking each day, and exercises at night, where I would lay down and raise my legs one at a time, heal to toe, raising them slowly, one at a time. I followed the recommendations and started to get well. In six months, I was back up to 136 pounds. I've been well ever since, and I still have the kidney, and the kidney operates fine.

As soon as I was well enough, I went to Virginia Beach to see this man. I think I had gotten the reading in January. I went to the Cayce home, and Mrs. Cayce answered the door and said, "Edgar's out there in the garden picking strawberries," so this had to be sometime in May. Mrs. Cayce was the most remarkable woman. She was kind, understanding, and the manner in which she handled the problems that confronted her always amazed me. There was a lot of people coming into that house, day in and day out, with all kinds of problems, but I never saw her ruffled.

I want to talk about Edgar Cayce. You see, at the time, the idea of Cayce's talents were new to most people. I was so intrigued. I wanted to get more psychic myself, and so one day I asked the question, "Can everyone become psychic?" And he said, "Yes, everyone can do the same thing, if you're willing to pay the price."

Let me tell you one of the things that happened to me. It seems like Mr. Cayce was always trying to work with me to get me to wake up my consciousness, or something. I had a bad argument with one of my neighbors, and I was real shook up about it. I was just as angry as I could be with her. If any of us in Study Group #1 had a problem, we just felt like we had to come down and talk to Mr. Cayce, as he was the one who could straighten these things out.

I came down, and he was sitting in the library reading a book. He looked up at me, for about a minute, and he got up and walked into his office and shut the door. Well, I sat there and waited for him for about ten or fifteen minutes. I had caught a ride into Virginia Beach with a friend, and I knew we were going back in a little bit so I went over and I knocked on the door and said,

"Mr. Cayce. I want to see you."

He said, "Go away, come back next week."

I said, "I've got to see you."

He said again, "Go away and come back next week."

Well, there wasn't anything else to do, so I left. When the time came for his Tuesday night Bible class, I got there a little bit early, and I sat in a chair next to where he sat to give the class. When he came in, I said, "What was the matter with you the other day? I needed to see you."

He said, "I didn't want to see you. I looked up at you and saw that aura was a flaming red color right up to the ceiling, and I wasn't about to get mixed up in that kind of anger." He knew exactly what had been going on.

There must have been a dozen or so of us that attended his Bible class regularly. We took turns taking notes of the class. Any of us that belonged to it, we wouldn't have missed that Bible class for anything. Robert Krajenke eventually used those notes we had taken as the basis for his book, *Edgar Cayce's Story of the Bible*. I joined the prayer group as soon as I found out about it. I was also a member of Study Group #1. Being in that first study group was an anchor to me. Here was something that you had to put into practice. You'd take one of these lessons, and you'd go home and study it, and you'd think you put it into practice and then you come back, and a reading was given and it would say, you better do it over again. You didn't put it into practice. Sometimes you knew within yourself that you hadn't done it and were just trying to get by.

Before I get into some of my family's personal readings, I remember the annual Congress group meeting for A.R.E. in 1940. Much of Europe was at war, and there was a great deal of concern about whether or not the United States would go to war, as well. The U.S. was running ships back and forth to England and many of us felt war might be inevitable. During that Congress, a reading was given on the topic of world affairs and what we might do to prepare for what was coming to America. The reading said that if the sixty-four of us present that day prayed and lived as we prayed, we could save America from being invaded. Although I know some of us wanted to dedicate ourselves to that goal, as I look back, I think we were just kind of jumping here and there. I don't think we really knew what that kind of dedication to God was all about—truly praying and living as you prayed.

In terms of my family, my son, Lorie, had physical readings and a life reading. It was through the physical readings that he overcame his asthma. His life reading occurred when he was two. The life reading said he should go into the field of communications. It also said that in his most recent lifetime he had been a lawyer and recommended that he should be trained in law—diplomatic law. It also said that he would deal with many countries and would have as a basis of operations places like Lima, Peru, Rio de Janeiro, Auckland, Buenos Aires, and so forth. It also said that he was very sensitive to places.

Well, being in the Navy, we moved around a lot. And my son did seem to be very opinionated about places. We'd come to a new place where we were supposed to live, and my son would say, "I'm not going in that house. I don't want to go into that house." Well, this was quite a problem and the reading had picked this up.

The reading had told me, "Give the entity a reason for everything you ask him to do." So I'd say, "Yes we need to go in there because this is our new house; we have to go in there. I can't stay out here because I have to go in and make us something to eat."

After thinking about it, Lorie would finally answer, "Well, I don't want to go in but I will." I tried to reason with him as often as I could.

When he got older and graduated from high school, he had a presidential appointment to Annapolis. He went in for a year in prep school and he came home and he said, "I don't want to be a naval officer." But he had to stay three years longer in the Navy.

I told him, "It's your life, you do what you want to do with it."

After the Navy, he went back to college and started in the field of communications, and graduated with a degree in electronics. He then went to work for four years at AT&T before going back to the University of Virginia. He transferred to William and Mary and got his degree there in law. He went to work for General Electric. This was for power line communication systems. He was also responsible for the site selection for the base of operations of a satellite station, as well as the frequency modulations. Certainly, his reading has come true in terms of the very broad field of communications. He now has contacts for power line communication systems in most of the areas that the reading said would be his base of operations: Rio de Janeiro, Lima, Africa, Spain, Mexico, Afghanistan, and so forth. He still follows his reading, and every once in a while he picks it up and says that he sees something else that he didn't see before.

There is an interesting story about my older son, Bruce. Bruce was about twenty when he met Mr. Cayce. When he had been a youngster, he had rheumatic fever, and as a result, he had a very bad heart. He was going to the University of Washington, and I wrote him to tell him about some of my dealings with Mr. Cayce. By this time, Harold and I had been transferred to Connecticut for a while, and so when Bruce came to see us, he was convinced that I had gotten mixed up in something funny. He said, "I want to see that old bird, Cayce, and find out what kind of charlatan you've gotten yourself involved with."

At that time, the government was drafting people and Bruce had tried to get into Army ROTC training, but the doctor had turned him down flat because of his heart and said, "No, we can't use you." The Coast Guard and the Navy turned him down, as well.

I asked Bruce, "How would you like to have a life reading?" Bruce thought it was a good idea just to see what this Cayce fellow was up to. So I called Mr. Cayce, and since we were up in Connecticut, Mr. Cayce said that Bruce was welcome to stay with them. So he went on down and stayed with the Cayces. He stayed with the Cayces for three days and it finally came time for his life reading.

The reading described him just perfectly. It said he was prone to stern judgment of others. It said he set his own boundaries and was prone to research what others claimed to be their experience. It said he was good with mathematics and was attracted to music and a good critic of music, all true, and then it said something that made Bruce think he had got him, after all. It said there was the necessity of him entering the army and being involved in engineering or communications.

Well, shortly after Bruce got back to Washington, his number came up and he was drafted. The same doctor that had turned him down for service in the first place examined him again and passed him.

Bruce asked him, "How come Doc, what about my heart?"

And the doctor said, "I don't see anything wrong

with your heart," and Bruce became a sergeant in the army.

Let me read you an excerpt from a letter that Bruce wrote Mr. Cayce a year later:

> Dear Mr. Cayce,
> It has been well over a year now since an afternoon in January that I shall always remember — an afternoon in which a whole new world opened to me. It has also been over a year since the day when I took off my civilian clothes for the uniform of the Army of the United States.
> In that year, Mr. Cayce, many things have happened to shape the forces which shall control my destiny. The job is not yet finished, nor will it ever be, yet there is a road ahead, and thanks to the greatness of some human souls, I have been given a map. A map, it is true, with which I am not too well acquainted; a map which I have not followed too closely; yet I know that as each day goes by, as each milestone is passed, the significance of what I have learned will become more and more important.
> Through the patience and confidence of my mother, and through the Corporation [A.R.E.], I have learned a new philosophy, a philosophy which is slowly crystallizing into a code, a way of life. It is true that I am slow — that always I have not followed that code — yet with each deviation, the ties become stronger — not weaker.
> If I do not write often, if at times you become worried about the worth of your work, know that I am one more friend among the thousands who will want to become more and more acquainted; yes, one who will want to become an active member when this war is over . . .
> Your work has certainly gone to better equip

one soldier, at least, for his job . . . In closing,
I wish to express my congratulations for the
book — *There Is a River*. Many of my friends
have shown a deep interest in your work,
and the book has been a wonderful source of
material for our discussions, which incidentally
are quite common in the barracks.

This was a kid that had always been a good boy but
hardheaded and always did just exactly what he wanted
to do.

My own life reading said I had abilities as a teacher,
as an instructor, and a writer. When I asked what I
should teach or write about it, it said, "The Book." When
I asked Mr. Cayce what he thought "The Book" meant,
he said, the Bible. It also said that I should help guide,
teach, and instruct young people.

Well, I have been teaching the story of Creation and
the Book of Genesis, as it exists in the readings for more
than thirty years. I also wrote the "Creation Trilogy,"
which has sold more than 50,000 copies. I still get letters
from people that say that this material has given them
an entirely new look and meaning to their lives.

In terms of guiding young people, I guess the way
this has mostly come about was through all of the work
I did with the so called "hippies" during the 1960s.
The way that some of these young people turned out,
it's marvelous. I had the opportunity to teach some
of these young people what has been shown to me
through the readings. Some of these young people
were mixed up with drugs. And sometimes they were
far out and all of these kinds of things that you can
say about them, but I noticed that there was a deep
searching in them. Whenever you could show them
that they were a part of God, and God was a part of
them, and you could make it clear to them, you could

make a difference. This is what I tried to do, to put it down on an everyday level where you could take a high spiritual concept and make it applicable to the person that you're speaking to. You could get them to understand who they were, where they came from, and how they got here. You didn't have to worry anymore about them. They straightened themselves out. This has been the major success that I've had so far with these young people.

Edgar and Gertrude Cayce were the most well balanced people that I've ever come in contact with — as individuals and as a couple. They were also very human. Edgar Cayce could get mad and fly off the handle but it didn't last very long — in a few minutes he was all over it. Mrs. Cayce would stand by and say, "Well, Edgar, I don't think you had to say that." She was the balance. These two people tried to keep an ideal of helping people. Their whole purpose seemed to be to make the world a better place in which to live. They were beautiful people.

## Chapter Twelve
## RUTH LENOIR

*Ruth LeNoir (1896-1981) met Edgar Cayce in 1931. Over the years, she received twelve personal readings from him on a variety of topics, as well as numerous group readings. She was an original member of the first A Search for God Study Group — Study Group #1, and an original member of the Glad Helpers Prayer group. She became Prayer Group secretary in 1950, a position she held until her death in 1981.*

*Fascinated by the Edgar Cayce information on the life of Jesus during the time of the Essenes, she compiled a book about that information entitled* When the Last Trumpet Is Sounded.

*This material is excerpted from Ruth's memories about her experiences with Edgar Cayce and the readings.*

The first time I ever heard of Edgar Cayce was through one of my sisters, who worked in an engraving and printing office in downtown Norfolk, Virginia. One day while we were having lunch together. She said to me, "We are making a booklet for a man who has just moved to Virginia Beach, and he does something very strange. If you are sick, he can go into a trance state and tell you what the trouble is and what to do about it."

I felt such a strong urge to meet this man that I said to my sister, "Can you get me one of those booklets?"

She told me it was called "A Man and His Work," and she would get me one, but she never did. Time passed, and I forgot about it.

Then another sister, who had built a home next door to mine, became pregnant. The doctor made a mistake and gave her something to stop the pains she was having, and she died within a week. The family had been called to the hospital at midnight, and when the nurse entered the room at five o'clock that morning to tell us that my sister had passed on, an inner voice said to me, "If you had known that man at Virginia Beach, your sister would not have died." The message was repeated a second time.

By the following spring, her house had been sold and new people had moved in, but I had not met them. One morning someone appeared at my front door and said to me, "I am your neighbor, and I have a daughter in the Cayce Hospital at Virginia Beach. She is due for a check reading, and I thought that maybe you would like to ride down to Virginia Beach with me?"

I felt that God was giving me a another chance to meet Edgar Cayce, so I accepted this wonderful opportunity at once. A desire of my heart was coming to pass, for I was most eager to listen to a reading by Edgar Cayce. This was to be my only visit to the Cayce Hospital before it closed.

After Edgar Cayce showed us around the hospital, we followed him to his home, where all the readings were given. Edgar Cayce and his wife, Gertrude, were warm and friendly people. I felt comfortable with them, as if I were meeting old friends.

Then Mr. Cayce proceeded to get ready to give the reading for my neighbor's daughter. His first step was to loosen his clothes—shoelaces, necktie, shirt cuffs, and belt—in order to have a perfectly free-flowing circulation. Then he lay down on the couch in his office. Once lying comfortably, he put both hands up to his forehead to the spot where observers had told him the third eye is located. Next he began to pray. Then he waited for a few minutes until he received the "go sign"—a flash of brilliant white light. After seeing the light, he moved both his hands down to his solar plexus, and his breathing became very deep. His eyes began to flutter and then closed. It was then that Gertrude Cayce gave him the suggestion. After listening to this reading I was most impressed! I thought that this was a man of God. Through all the years which have followed, I have never changed my mind.

At first, Edgar Cayce was crushed as he saw his dream of the hospital vanish, but after the hospital folded I was invited to join his A Search for God Study Group Program. The purpose of the program was to learn how to apply the spiritual lessons in the readings in our own lives, and then to share what we had learned with others. Many, many readings were given by Edgar Cayce on each lesson before that lesson was finally compiled. As I tried to live each lesson, definite results came from my activity, and the way was made easier. I have gained something for myself, which has made life much more worthwhile. For me, the Study Group Program has been twelve lessons in soul development.

In these readings, there are many thoughts that are worthy of careful examination. There are many suggestions for ways of thinking, for ways of changing your attitude, etc. There is also the strong encouragement to make prayer and meditation a part of your daily life. You must learn to meditate just as you have learned to do other things. Repeated effort soon becomes a habit, and habit then becomes second nature. This program has worked miraculous changes in the mental and emotional lives of those individuals who have tried it.

Sometimes we were too lax in our application, or we just didn't understand how to apply it but then we tried a little harder. The whole purpose of Edgar Cayce's life was to help people find their God. That is the heart of the Study Group Program. About a year after going to the Study Group meetings, I was asked if I would like to join in on the healing work of the Glad Helpers Prayer Group. The process of bringing healing to others through prayer involves raising the Christ Consciousness in self as well as awakening that consciousness in the individual who has asked for prayers. Both of these groups have meant the world to me.

So often we go through life hoping for a better world, but are we really doing anything about it? Until we awaken out of our sleep and make practical application of the things that we know, we'll never make very much progress. I have many examples of how the readings proved to be helpful in my own life but let me tell you two stories, both concerning my daughter, Jeanne.

One summer day, I awoke with a frightful dream. I saw a cemetery and in the cemetery there was a new grave. Somehow I could see through the dirt into the coffin, and in the coffin I saw my daughter. I tried to shake myself from what I had seen, for it was a real nightmare.

At the time, we lived in a small cottage not too far from the ocean. Jeanne was fourteen, and had been in the habit of putting on her bathing suit to go swimming each morning, but for some reason, there were several days in a row where she didn't go swimming—instead she just stayed on the porch and read. One afternoon, she fell sound asleep on the porch. A neighbor from one of the cottages nearby came over to see me, passing Jeanne on the porch. She had been trained as a nurse. When she got inside, she said, "I don't want to alarm you, but I think Jeanne has typhoid fever. I have nursed many cases, and the fever has a peculiar odor."

Typhoid fever? I thought she had to be wrong. Whoever hears of typhoid fever anymore? When we took her temperature, however, it was 104 degrees. Completely shaken, I went to the phone and called Virginia Beach for a reading. The reading was set for the next morning. Later that day, the doctor came over and diagnosed Jeanne's case as having pus on her kidneys. He gave her a prescription and the fever subsided a bit.

Hugh Lynn Cayce called me the next morning as soon as the reading was given. Cayce had diagnosed the condition as typhoid fever. The readings went on to say that her condition was serious but a course of treatment was recommended. It also recommended massages each day with grain alcohol to help reduce the fever. I put Jeanne's name on the prayer list, as prayer help was important to me as part of the treatment. Jeanne did not get well immediately. There were times when she was so sick that she couldn't even raise her arm off the bed. Several nights I was so alarmed about her condition that I sat on the bed beside her, held her hand and just prayed. Once she started crying and weakly asked me to get another reading, "Mother, I don't want to die!"

We did get another reading and it gave us both encouragement. It said that conditions were showing much improvement. New information was given on diet, and osteopathic treatments were added. One member of the prayer group came to sit up with Jeanne at night, so I could get some sleep. Through all this time, the doctor kept coming by the house to check on Jeanne. I didn't know how to stop him from coming. He didn't know exactly what we were doing to help her but he would just look her over and say, "Well, keep up the treatments. She seems to be doing fine." Before long, Jeanne returned to complete health.

I have often told the other story about Jeanne. It happened after she had gone off to attend college at William and Mary in Williamsburg, Virginia. At the time, I was living two hours away in Charlottesville, Virginia. Jeanne was trying to climb into her bed at college, which was on the upper bunk. She had climbed on the back of a chair, slipped, and hit her spine on the way down. By the next morning, she couldn't get out of bed and was taken to the infirmary. Her roommate called me at around 10 a.m. and told me what had happened. She said the doctor was with her and would call as soon as he was able.

He called me soon afterwards and said that Jeanne was very uncomfortable and could barely move. He was worried about a spinal injury, and said that paralysis was a definite possibility. He asked if I wanted him to call our family doctor. The only doctor I wanted to call was Edgar Cayce. However, I knew that with all the publicity Mr. Cayce had gotten of late, his appointment book was filled for at least a year in advance. Obviously, we couldn't wait that long. A reading for Jeanne was needed right now.

I made the call from Charlottesville to Virginia Beach. Harmon Bro answered the phone. He told me that Mr. Cayce had already started his morning readings. Gertrude and Gladys were with him, and they could not be disturbed. He explained that there were so many readings scheduled that he didn't think it could be gotten today but he would tell Mr. Cayce about Jeanne later. I didn't know what to do. I was so confused that I prayed for guidance. I paced all morning and through the afternoon. I prayed as I paced. Finally, I couldn't wait any longer. I placed another call to Virginia Beach; this time, Gladys Davis answered the phone.

I blurted out, "Gladys, is there any way in the world I can get a reading for Jeanne?"

Her answer came as a complete surprise: "We got it this morning; I have already mailed it to Jeanne at college." She said that Mr. Cayce had volunteered the information at the end of three other readings. He hadn't even been given the suggestion about Jeanne! Asleep on the couch he had suddenly said, "Charlottesville — Williamsburg," and proceeded to say, "Now we have the conditions with Jeanne . . ." The information had come through right after my call with Harmon. Somehow, he had picked up on my worry in Charlottesville, and tuned into Jeanne in Williamsburg. He outlined the regimen of treatment and then added at the end of the reading, "We haven't made a mistake," apparently responding to the thoughts of someone in the room.

Jeanne was in so much pain that I had a very hard time getting her out of school so that I could follow the reading, but I got her. The infirmary at the school wasn't doing anything for her. They were just keeping her quiet, and she was getting stiffer all the time. Rather than going back to Charlottesville, I took her into Norfolk, Virginia to the home of a friend of mine who could help me with the treatments. We followed the treatments for three days and she returned to school. She has never had any trouble since.

One of the things that I learned from the Study Group readings was that as long as we lived as we prayed, we could ask for anything we really needed and it would be given. The Study Group Program also seemed to enhance practical experiences with intuition, just like Mr. Cayce said were available to us. After my divorce, I often had many troubles and one of those was money. There were times when I was filled with confusion, doubt, and fear. I was trying to raise a daughter and was in a real need of money, and I prayed that God would show me the way. One morning, I awoke just somehow knowing that before the day was over, I would receive a certain amount of cash. It wasn't a large sum but it was an amount that I needed very much. I looked at the morning paper and quickly ran through the "Help Wanted" pages until I found an ad that I thought I could deal with. The ad was placed by the American Automobile Association (AAA).

I got on a bus and was in Norfolk by 9 a.m., and went directly to the AAA office. They were advertising for salespeople to sell memberships, and about a dozen people had showed up that morning in response to the ad. The first thing the manager did was to give us a pep talk. Then he announced that on this first day we were being sent out with no leads, no names, and no prospects. We were to try and sell these memberships on our own. All of a sudden, I felt completely helpless.

I was disappointed by the turn of events and left the office with the others. I crossed over to one of the main places where buses passed every few minutes. I stood there, and started enjoying the feeling of the warm spring morning and the sunshine. I let myself feel the beauty of the day. My feeling of helplessness melted away.

One of the provisions in the AAA membership enthused me, it stated that a member was entitled to help with bail in case of an accident in which they were arrested away from home. The manager had stressed this point in his talk. I thought it was a very strong selling point. As I stood there waiting for the bus, I kept wishing that I knew somebody who was going to travel. I couldn't think of a single person. Standing there in that busy thoroughfare, I asked for God's help and promised that wherever he led me, I would follow. I prayed with one of the prayers I had learned from the Prayer Group. I decided that I was going to stand there until the spirit moved me from within. I stood and waited; I waited quite a while. I kept prayerful, and I tried to keep my mind from wandering or feeling anxious. All at once, I felt a gentle urge to "get on THIS bus." I got on, not knowing where the bus was headed.

It turned out to be a bus that went way out of town. When I reached the end of the line, I was still on it. I hadn't yet had any feeling of direction as to where I should get off. I prayed some more, got off, and found myself on a road called Cedar Lane. At first, I wasn't certain which way to go, but I crossed the road and started walking down the street. I gazed intently at the first house but decided to pass it on. I skipped the second house, too. When I got to the third house, I turned right in, walked up to the front, and rang the bell. The house somehow "felt right."

A gentleman opened the door, and I introduced myself as a salesperson for AAA. He said, "I was just getting ready to pick up the telephone and call your office. We've planned a trip, but I wouldn't think of leaving without membership for my wife and I in the American Automobile Association." He was particularly concerned because a friend of his had been on a trip and had become involved in an accident. "So I want two memberships—one for my wife and one for myself." I couldn't wait to get back to the office, so I used the man's phone to let them know right then and there. For me, the story illustrates that somewhere within each of us there is a wellspring of faith that we can draw upon.

I am often asked how the Cayce readings have helped me. The idea of reincarnation was completely new to me, but it has helped me a great deal. The readings gave me a new philosophy to live by, and that is to do all I can to be of help to other people. I was led to the realization that God's laws are unchangeable, and by practicing to be a part of His Presence, I could overcome loneliness and disappointment and awaken new hope. Gradually, into my consciousness came a feeling of peace and security and the ability to carry on. I have come to understand that God continually seeks expression through each of us, we just have to set our selfishness aside. Ultimately, I think, the readings gave me a clearer understanding of God, who had never been real to me before.

## Chapter Thirteen
# WILFRED ("BILL") SECHRIST

*Bill Sechrist (1909-1987) had a career primarily in corporate management. He was a flight-test engineer for Bendix Aviation Corporation during World War II, and later was a marketing and management executive with internationally known manufacturers.*

*Bill had a lifelong involvement in community and civic causes. Bill was especially interested in the moral, vocational, and business aspects of the Cayce readings. Together with his wife, Elsie, he lectured throughout the world, often conferring with international experts in the fields of parapsychology and metaphysics. Bill personally underwrote the couple's many decades of international travels, disseminating the Cayce information around globe.*

*Known for his business acumen and his sense of humor, this is adapted from an interview Bill gave in 1984 and an A.R.E. Congress lecture in 1986.*

I guess my first encounter with Edgar Cayce was through my wife, Elsie. While we were living in New York, she was very interested in Edgar Cayce and all that was going on down here in Virginia Beach. It got so bad that if I wanted to see her, I had to come to Virginia Beach to do so. I met Mr. Cayce at the time, and we became good friends. He was a joy to have around. We shared some interests. We shared a love of fishing and an interest in photography. He had a great affinity for and with children.

He and I did not delve into the esoteric to the extent that he and Elsie did. One time, we were sitting out there on the lawn, and he looked at me. I've forgotten exactly how he put it, but he said, "You don't exactly go for all of this stuff." And he made that as a statement, not a question. And then he added to that, he says, "Well, that's a good approach. You like to see proof; you like to have proof, and that's good."

I saw him more often in New York than I did down in Virginia Beach. We hosted him in New York. I also counseled with him about business on the conscious level. He was a very brilliant man even though he didn't trust his conscious advice. He was always afraid he would make a mistake. And I had some business readings. I can truthfully say that his business readings, not only mine but those I have read belonging to others, helped me to form a business philosophy. Following the philosophy contained in his readings certainly contributed probably 75 to 80 percent of my success in the business world.

I think that the basic principle Edgar Cayce preached is one that, if adhered to, can help us throughout, and that is the Golden Rule: *Do unto others as you would have them do unto you.* That runs through so many of his readings. He talked about cooperation in business, trying to help the other fellow. Don't be willing just to meet the other fellow halfway. If necessary, go 90 percent of the way or 95 percent of the way. Work with prayer. Hold to the right ideals. He gave many examples of this throughout the readings.

Before World War II ended, I was concerned about what I was going to do when the war was over, and I asked a question in one reading, "How may I best carry on after the end of World War II in order to not interrupt my spiritual growth?" I guess I was assuming at the time that I would grow spiritually. And he said, "Don't worry about this. All you have to do is do the very best that you know how, and it will carry you. You won't have to do anything." I asked him about what company I should become associated with after the war was over, and he said any company that has a heart. And he says, specifically, "General Electric has a heart, Bendix has a heart," and I was with Bendix Aviation at the time. Elsie and I were the recipients of the bounty of that big-hearted Bendix Aviation the likes of which you can't imagine.

Cayce also highlights the importance of working with your dreams in business. I could elaborate on that for several hours. I never had a problem with an employee, especially a key employee, an executive employee, that I didn't dream about it weeks or even months before the experience came. If an employee was unhappy, sometimes I would know it even before the employee knew it. I would see it in a dream.

Why would I dream that an employee is going to leave us, leave my company? It is twofold. Number one, I think it was because it was giving me an opportunity to counsel the employee. And I did that. I'd have a talk with the employee and ask, "Why are you leaving? Do you have a better opportunity?" Analyze the reason the employee is leaving. Is it going to be best for that employee to leave? And in many instances, it would be. Maybe the employee is stymied where they are at. If so, tell them to go on and take advantage of the opportunity. The second reason I think dreams gave me a forewarning of an employee's departure was so that I could be making plans to fill the slot that the employee left vacant. This is just putting it into practice. Dreams can truly help with employee relationships. I was also warned in my dreams about employees who were dishonest, for example.

Back to meeting Edgar Cayce. Elsie and I both had physical readings first, because who can argue with the fact if he tells you that you have a problem or that you don't have a problem, and you know that is the case? So, we thought, before the life readings, we would go for the physical readings. And in my physical reading, for example, he found many things that I knew were right, and he found many things that I knew were bothersome to me.

For example, I was prone to sinus problems — sinusitis. I was also given to migraine headaches. He said that these were having to do with upset in the lymph system. He put me on a routine of colonic irrigations, electrical current applications, massage, steam baths, fume baths, and so forth. Fortunately, we were living in New York City, and it was just a matter of going over to Reilly's Health Institute and getting it. I started a friendship with Reilly back in 1942 or '43. After I started these physical treatments through Reilly, I began to show immediate improvement. I think within a matter of probably a year, I forgot what a migraine headache was all about, and here I had had those for years. They started when I was just a teenager.

Let me add something right there. I had my physical reading in the early 1940s. In 1970, I retired from business. And when I retired, I came apart. I became all unglued as it were. Elsie and I had been on an extended trip. I came back to this country, and I was suffering from acute prostatitis. I was suffering from acute hypertension, and I had some serious things wrong with me, as well. I was scheduled for major surgery in our home down in Houston. Elsie said, "No way. We'll go up to the A.R.E. Clinic in Phoenix." We went to the clinic. Dr. Bill McGarey started me out on another routine of physical therapy. The first thing we did was to call Gladys Davis Turner back in Virginia Beach and have her send my readings out. Bill incorporated my Cayce readings from decades earlier into my therapy! And I never had the surgery. I'm in pretty fair shape for the condition that I'm in.

Before I briefly mention my life reading, let me give you a little bit of my religious background. I was born into the most dogmatic of religions. Essentially, you were conceived in sin, you were born in sin, you lived in sin, and you unquestionably died in sin. There was no doubt that you would burn in the fires of Hell forever. With this as my background, religion was not for me, simply not for me. I left the church when I was fifteen or sixteen. Didn't go back in again. Elsie and I were twenty-seven, or so, I think, when we start looking for some spiritual direction. We started going to a teacher in New York City back in 1937. This fellow was quite good. He proposed the idea of reincarnation, and for me everything fell into place. That was the whole answer to the whole thing. Nothing else had made sense up to that time. The old version of you were born, you live, and you die, and that's it, and then you get to strum a harp or shovel coal throughout eternity, didn't make any sense to me. But this idea of being reborn and being able to grow and improve yourself enabled everything to fall into place.

I think that I am proof today of many lifetimes. It reminds me of the story of the two girls who were talking and one of them said to the other, "There must be something to this reincarnation bit. I could never have made such a mess of my life in just one lifetime." I think my life has had some bearing on this. I don't think

I have learned in this one lifetime all that I know, what I sense, and what I believe is right. My various abilities and my various interests are an accumulation of what I've been in all my previous lifetimes. And I think my Cayce readings prove that—the highlights that he touched upon.

I won't go into all of the details or lifetimes of my life reading, but Cayce said that I had abilities as an engineer. He said that if I chose, I could earn my living as an engineer. When World War II came along, I was with Evinrude Outboard Motors. Some of you may know about them. We thought we were going to be out of business because of the war effort, so they said, "Go on, Bill, get a job somewhere else and after the war is over, come back to us." I got a job as a laboratory technician with Bendix Aviation Corporation. A laboratory technician means you clean up the benches after the engineers get through with them.

I had been there just six months, and they were having courses every day—refresher courses for the engineers. I would sit in those courses, an hour and a half every day at noontime. At the end of six months' time, I had been promoted to a Developmental Engineer both in rank, title, and salary. I had no engineering background. I had had three years of vocational school. Everything else had been marketing prior to that time.

During that period, Mr. Cayce said that if I chose to, I could be successful as an engineer, but he indicated that I would also go back into marketing, which I did. I was offered an opportunity to stay in engineering sales. I liked to sell. He said that my ability as a salesman stemmed from a previous incarnation in old Persia, in a city in the hills and plains near a place called Shushtar. He said this was once a center of healing and trade and learning, where people came from all over the known world. According to my reading, I had a camel caravan route between Egypt and India. If you know that part of the country, the caravan routes came around the southern end of the Red Sea, came across what is now Jordan down into India. That's where I learned to sell pots and pans, which came in handy later on when I worked with marketing for Presto Pressure Cooker. That's where I learned about silk and materials and so forth. That's where I learned the love of camels.

You know, the first time that Elsie and I went to Shushtar, we were staying at this Inn, and that night, I had a dream where I relived my experience in old Persia — the one that Cayce had given a reading about. And it was in that dream where I realized that it had been in the Persian lifetime where I first came in contact with this idea of reincarnation, and that's why it came so easy to me in the present.

The first time I ever saw a herd of camels, I got so excited I nearly wrecked the car. We were driving down in the backside of Jordan. We'd gotten ourselves in a mess down there and saw this herd of camels. I never did get my camera so I could get a picture of them. Finally got a telephoto lens, and I got the most wonderful picture of the south end of a northbound herd of camels that you ever saw. But today, I know what a camel is thinking. I have no problem with a camel. Elsie walks up to a camel, and it starts to snarl and spit, but my rapport with camels is just great.

According to my life reading, Elsie was my mother during the Persian period. She hitchhiked a ride from the lowlands of India to this city, where she remained for the rest of her life. She would never have gotten there if I hadn't given her a free ride from India.

As important as the physical reading and the life reading were to me, I think being involved in the spiritual growth material and study groups has just been immeasurably helpful. Let me tell you a story. We had been in study groups for five years—prayer, meditation, dreams, the whole bit. Elsie had started the first study group in New York, and when we got to Los Angeles, we were in a study group, as well. But after we got to Los Angeles, nothing was happening. Everything was just remaining rather status quo. Even in the study group, I felt like I wasn't seeing any progress. I felt like Elsie and I had reach a low point in our lives.

I was out of a job. We were living in a two-room garage apartment. Our furniture was in storage in a broken down warehouse in the Watts district. We had a broken-down car, and we were in debt thousands of dollars that we had borrowed from a friend of ours just to live on. I complained about the situation we were in many times to Elsie, and her response was always, "You know, God's arm is not short." Eventually, I started to reply, "Not only is it short, but it's broken in two places."

One night, I was at my lowest point. Elsie was already in bed and had turned off her night table light. I made a statement as I was going to bed that I didn't know why I bothered anymore. Here I had been keeping a dream journal for almost five years. I had been meditating, and I had been praying, but no one was listening. After saying that, I felt pretty good because I had gotten it off my chest. I went to sleep and had a pretty good night's rest.

I awoke the next morning after making that forlorn statement. The room's window was quite high, and I looked out through these tall palm trees at this very blue California sky. As I looked, there appeared in the sky this solid gold ear, perfect in every dimension, about 200 feet tall. I stared and stared at it for quite a while. As I looked at that ear, a feeling of euphoria filled every cell in my body, because I absolutely knew without a doubt that somebody was listening.

Right after that, I continued just as I had been doing. I was sending out resumes. I was making telephone calls. I was going for interviews—jumping around anywhere that I could to have an interview, but I was doing it with a different attitude, and I am sure my attitude showed in my face. A short time later, I was offered the most wonderful position that I had had up to that time, working with the most wonderful group of people that you could ever become associated with. Before the year was out, Elsie and I had a nice home again, our furniture was around us, we had paid off our indebtedness to our friend, we were able to finance two new cars, and we've never been down since. That was an answer to a prayer.

I want to talk a minute, if I may, about this idea of the profit motive. Money is no curse. The curse comes with what you do with it. Elsie and I are able to travel the whole world at will. We do not travel cheaply. Believe me, we enjoy the finer things, the better things of life. And every bit of this has come about through guidance that we've had in dreams in how to make investments, what to do with our money, how to do it. And if the profit motive is wrong, I don't think we would have had these profits that we've had.

I think that Edgar Cayce and his work has enabled me to lead—if there is such a phrase—a contented life, never satisfied, but I've been happy. I've been happy in my life and in my work. I've been happy because I've understood what I was doing. I had a basic philosophy, which honestly came from Edgar Cayce that has seen me through.

*Chapter Fourteen*
# HARMON H. BRO

*Harmon H. Bro, Ph.D. (1919-1997) was a psychotherapist, a teacher, a writer, an ordained minister, and an inspirational lecturer. As a young man, he lived and worked in the Cayce home during the last portion of Edgar Cayce's life and witnessed several hundred readings. His books about Cayce's life and work include* Edgar Cayce: A Seer Out of Season *and* Edgar Cayce on Religion, Spirituality, and Psychic Experience.

*This is a compilation of a lecture Harmon gave at A.R.E.'s 19th annual Congress and an interview from 1975.*

People each have their own special way of telling this story, and of course mine begins with *There Is a River*, which had just recently been published. I read it when I was a night guard with a gun on my hip at the Manhattan Project at the University of Chicago, earning extra money so I could get married. My mother had just written a review for the Cayce biography and had been to Virginia Beach to meet Cayce for herself. Afterwards, she came to Chicago and we met for lunch.

She told the story of her visit with Edgar Cayce, and I really was quite concerned that this fairly stable woman, effective at upper echelons of church work, an editor and so on, might have slipped somehow. I thought she might have "gone off her rocker" — or so it seemed. She was preparing to do an article for *Coronet* magazine on Cayce's work.

I was still concerned, not long afterwards, when I got a life reading for myself. I couldn't help but wonder whether Edgar Cayce had been influenced by my mother, because I was heading for a career in church music, and he insisted I should work in the theological world, which seemed to be much more like my mother than me.

Six years later, in May 1949, I turned in at the largest divinity school in the world — the Federated Theological Schools of the University of Chicago — a six-hundred-page manuscript. It was my dissertation for the Ph.D. degree, and it was about — you guessed it — Edgar Cayce!

Now I want to share with you some of the insights I got during those six years of work — insights into who Edgar Cayce was, what he was like, and what kind of challenge he presents to us who know about him.

With a little coaxing, I came down to Virginia Beach in late 1943 and went to work on the staff of the Association for Research and Enlightenment, observing first-hand everything that went on during what proved to be the last year of Mr. Cayce's life. I got a chance to come to Virginia Beach as a gift from Myrtle Walgreen, who had been here.

Once I got to Virginia Beach, my thinking was that I could help Cayce discriminate what was valid for his time and what wasn't. My job was to try, as best I could, to figure out what his son, Hugh Lynn, had been doing and to do some of it. I came in with all the cockiness I suppose that a second year graduate student has to have. I thought he was wasting his time giving all of these readings for individuals — wouldn't it be better to give readings on illnesses themselves? I thought there wasn't enough structure to Cayce's schedule—maybe certain days should be set aside for certain kinds of readings. It also seemed to me that certain types of readings should take precedence over other types. Finally, when I had the opportunity during a reading, I asked him a series of questions.

Question: "Would it be advisable to give mental and spiritual readings precedence over physical readings?"

Answer: "Would the Master make precedence of physical, of mental? He took them as they came. Pretty good pattern to follow!"

I next asked the question, "Should a definite proportion of our time go to physical readings, life readings, mental and spiritual readings? For instance, two days each week for each class of problems?"

Answer: "As the Lord moved them, so were they added."

Finally I asked the question, "What is the maximum number of readings which should be handled in one day?"

The answer was short and to the point, "What business is that of yours? We are through."

I had come to Virginia Beach with a lot of ideas in my mind, a lot of things I expected to find because I had read *There Is a River*, and talked to a few people, and had a life reading. But in just about every case, I was wrong in what I expected.

For example, I expected to demonstrate that the physical readings were rather inefficient, that they were picking up a very low level of medical information. They were dealing with herbs and paths and packs and some devices . . . I felt that if someone could help Mr. Cayce really focus his ability, he would pick out the big-name drugs and some other valuable things. Well,

I found the physical readings a lot sounder than I had dreamed.

Then, I expected to see some pretty good clairvoyant stunts, a few of them, when I got down there. For this guy, Cayce, was supposed to be able to pick up a few thoughts here and there, and even to describe things at a distance. As a matter of fact, I soon saw thousands of clairvoyant "stunts" for I heard things in those readings — as I sat there day by day with my notebook — that bowled me over again and again. Frequently, I dropped my jaw, dropped my pencil, picked up both and had to start again. It was incredible, the things this fellow described, lying there on that couch asleep. I recall the time he gave a reading for a man in California; it was early in the morning out there and Mr. Cayce began the reading with a humorous aside, "Mmm, right nice looking pajamas!" By the time I had put together little things like that with all of the serious details in the readings I heard, I had witnessed an awful lot of clairvoyance — more than I ever expected.

Thirdly, I expected to find Edgar Cayce going through some sort of a rigmarole in getting ready to give his readings; you know, maybe incense or special postures and gestures — there had to be something screwy! But I got here, and there wasn't anything of the sort. He just walked into his study, sat down, talked a little while, then he was quiet a little while, and then he lay down and went to sleep. I was disappointed again.

Well, I thought, surely this man is human enough to have a weakness about money. All of the people that I'd ever met with any unusual talent capitalized on it when they got the opportunity. I figured Edgar Cayce would do that too. He didn't. I'd examine the letters that came in — there'd be money in them, just a gift because someone liked what he was doing. He'd say, "Put it back. Send it back. We don't take money except for memberships, and we don't encourage memberships unless people are in need of some real service." And back the money would go—hundreds and hundreds of dollars in the many *Coronet* letters. How that startled me! Later on, I discovered further that he wasn't even collecting membership fees from many of the people who joined the Association and asked for readings; if they didn't send the money, he didn't insist on it. That knocked me over. Here was a man with utter integrity, who never went grasping for money on the basis of his unusual gift.

I expected a man who would at least pose as a saint. Who could have such a gift and not feel that the divine had somehow settled specially over him? I expected a guy who would claim never to make mistakes, who would be a meticulous ascetic—a perfect example of all the right things, you know? Well, he didn't pose as a saint, never claimed to be one. He laughed whenever you talked to him about that, said he only hoped his work might "cover a multitude of sins." He kidded about the way he smoked cigarettes continually, liked to eat plenty, enjoyed having a good time with people. Never claimed to be a saint. That surprised me.

I expected also, to tell the truth, a very simple person, because I got the impression from reading his biography that this man was a victim of circumstances, one who had a gift happen to him and just drifted along, one thing batting on him after another—a very simple person. Well, I found that I was wrong there, too. A keen mind, strong convictions, a strong will, many facets to his personality. A dramatic speaker. All kinds of things in the man that I never expected.

Lastly, I thought that in his religious life I'd probably find kind of a traditional, Sunday School religion. You know, kind of a small-town, peaceful, external, church-going religion in his personal life. I was wrong again! Religion, experience of God, was a deep river in his life. One little occasion symbolized it for me so well that I have long remembered it. Someone called him up one night, a mother, and said, "My little boy's getting well. We followed the directions in your reading and he's okay now; but he was very sick." When Mr. Cayce hung up the phone, he told me about it and then he walked to his office. I started out of the building. It happened that I'd forgotten something, and I came back in; he didn't know that I returned, and there he was back in his office, where I could hear him saying, "Thank you, God. Thank you, God. Thank you, God." All alone, by himself, back there. That moment showed me some things.

I sat in on a great many readings; I think I heard about 500. My wife, June, and I lived in an apartment in a Navy place some distance away, but we were invited cordially and happily into the family circle for Sunday dinners and for group meetings. We were always at the Sunday Bible class and the Tuesday evening Bible class, or study group in the home. We always felt a genuine part of the operation, but it was pretty rattled with so much activity. There were sixteen secretaries at the time, and the place was crammed with mail. It was stacked up waist high all through the dining room and the library and the study and portions of Mr. Cayce's office.

Gertrude, as I recall her, was always gracious to me and to many others. She had almost a regal bearing about her in a composed and quiet way. She could be genuinely warm. What she was on the surface, she was also inside. Edgar Cayce could be very open and very outgoing and very glowing at times, but she was a little more reserved until she was sure who she was with and what their spirit was, and then everything was yours. I don't remember her ever getting ruffled, even with all that was going on. Often she would loosen everybody up before a reading was being given with some cute little story. Whenever she walked through the room, there was always a smile. They was always an attempt to keep people on an even keel. She was always on top of the routine of things.

I love the memory of both Mr. and Mrs. Cayce showing me and many others the photographs on the wall above Mr. Cayce's couch and on the other wall. They savored these people. They were sad over those who had experienced sadness in their lives; glad over those who had succeeded.

I found Cayce easy to talk with even from the beginning. His major mode of relating to people in words initially was to tell stories, and this both conveyed him in a good way, and also took some of the tension off of people inspecting him, which everyone was doing initially. And it also protected him a little bit. He didn't have to disclose his own depths while he was telling the story. He could just be in the story and in the human experience.

Because the stress was so great, after supper he was often back there in his office, pecking out letters on that little typewriter. Early in the morning, after his devotional time, more often than not he was also typing out these letters. These were not just to friends and to people who had had readings, many were to strangers who had requested help.

I came to see him as a most talented man in many, many areas. I looked at it in his photographs. It was there when he wrote and thought out his compositions. It was evident in his lecturing, and it was extraordinarily clear in his telling of stories, and, of course, it was evident in the readings.

I was impressed as everyone with his knowledge of
the Bible. I sometimes teased him. I knew it as a graduate
student, and I would at times start him off in Kings or
Psalms or something and just for fun, I would watch him
continue the passage. My sense of the importance of his
dealing with the Bible is not what he knew. There was
no sense of fundamentalist in the sense of just using the
Bible to make points and quotes. This was a thoughtful
man who dealt with biblical quotes and questions
like sin, and grace, and hope, and guidance. He drew
a picture of a level of human existence in relationship
with God, which was decisive for those who were in
his classes and groups. There is a way to walk your
journey with God and not simply to be obedient but to
be tremendously alive, and open, and repentant, and
hopeful, and creative. The picture he drew was that all
these people had walked with God, and you can too.

I began to learn that everything about Edgar Cayce
was religious, God-related, as far as he could make it. His
greatest weekly joys came in teaching his Bible classes,
one at his home and one at the Presbyterian Church; his
heart was in it. He did his counseling—and plenty of
people came to talk with him apart from his readings
—on the basis of the Bible and its great promises and
challenges. His readings he said he would only give so
long as they brought Christ nearer to the people that
had them. He'd quit, he said, as soon as the readings
failed to make people feel that.

Edgar Cayce lived and worked right here in Virginia
Beach, and it looks as though he was one of the most
highly gifted religious seers in recorded history. Edgar
Cayce appears unique. He did more, for more people,
over a longer period of time than anybody we yet
know about in recorded history with this particular
type of gift. The range of his vision—health problems,

vocational problems, past lives, philosophical truths, mental attitudes, historical facts—there's no evidence now of other seers who could see all this. And there's the religious maturity of what he said, the deeply ethical framework in which counsel was handed out, the concern for God's will that stood behind whatever he said and challenged whomever he guided. Then there's the simplicity of what he did as a seer. He just served, and served, and served, so simply.

What does it mean? A lot of strange things happening? It looks, rather, as though God got awfully tired of waiting around for us to wake up. He pulled the curtains aside a little bit and let some light shine through. A lot of light; an awful lot of it! He picked a soul that had plenty of puzzles to solve, plenty of karma to meet, but He trusted him and He gave him the job to do. Edgar Cayce did it. Do you know what I think it all means? I think it means this: that God cares. That He cares about us, that no matter how busy we are, or how crazy we are, of how self-centered we are, He hasn't given us up.

What shall we do with this man, Edgar Cayce? Shall we go around telling his story? Sure, we tell his story; we've got to tell his story. It's like high voltage electricity—unless you pass it along, it'll burn you alive. But that's not enough. God doesn't really need publicity; He isn't just asking us to handle His public relations.

Do we start changing society on the basis of Edgar Cayce's work? Sure we do. I'm going to pitch into the Christian church with all the strength I have. I have a psychologist friend who is a Cayce enthusiast already at work changing psychological theories as much as he can; the rest of you can help change these things and can change a great many things: medicine, politics, education, diet patterns, your own home, and much more on the basis of what came through the readings.

But all of this is not enough. God doesn't seek merely a different society; He knows He has no society any better than the people in it. What He wants is changed lives! And He wants them from us. That is what we do with Edgar Cayce.

We've got to be different, very different. Someday you and I are going to hear a voice, a very disturbing voice, that's going to say, "I let you in on Edgar Cayce; what did you do with him?" And we're going to have to answer. We're going to want to have changed. Through the readings of Edgar Cayce, we can be helped to see ourselves and to see how far we are from what God wants us to be. Then we can be different; we must be different. People can see it in our faces when we start wiping out some of the selfishness. We have to be so changed that people will see it, and know it.

When you get stuck, when you forget the real challenge of Edgar Cayce's work, of this religious seer and his gift, turn to these words—words that came at the end of so many life readings. Pin them over your heart:

> **Study to show thyself approved, a workman not ashamed, rightly dividing the words of truth, keeping self unspotted from the world. For know, thy God has given thee much; He does expect much from thee.**

## Chapter Fifteen
# THOMAS SUGRUE

*Thomas Sugrue (1907-1953) met Hugh Lynn Cayce at college, and came to Virginia Beach in 1927 to get a reading from Cayce's father, Edgar Cayce. Over the next sixteen years, Sugrue would have more than seventy readings of his own. He would write the only Cayce biography that was published during Edgar Cayce's lifetime,* There Is a River, *which has acquainted countless individuals with the Cayce work and has sold more than one million copies.*

*The author of numerous books, Sugrue also wrote for* The New York Times, *served as a reporter with the* New York Herald Tribune *and a staff writer with the* American Magazine, *and was the author of hundreds of articles and book reviews. He frequently loaned his writing talents to A.R.E. and wrote the booklet "A Man and His Work," describing Cayce's work.*

*This material is adapted from Thomas Sugrue's written memories, as well as his address to the 10th Annual A.R.E. Congress.*

It was my fortune, when in my youth, to have conversations with a very good listener, Hugh Lynn Cayce, who smiled tolerantly at my rudimentary philosophies. I had many questions of life that troubled me. Through long nights of the 1926 winter in Lexington,

Virginia, in our tiny rooms in Lee's Dormitory, when we
should have been preparing lessons for the stern masters
of Washington and Lee University, we talked.

One night, he told me, "My father is a psychic."

It is now a long time since that happened, and I do not
remember much, except that we stayed up all night and
that at breakfast we were still talking. I wanted to know
more, but I did not believe. I was a Roman Catholic
Irishman from Connecticut. He was a Christian Church
member from Virginia. There was no valid reason why
we should like each other, why we should be together.
It was, I thought afterward, almost indecent.

He talked of a God who was merciful, who was
understanding, who saw eye to eye with my blundering
desires in life. So we forsook sleep on other nights, and
talked again, and again. He told me of a man, his father,
who lay down to sleep and spoke with the voice of
authority: who cured the halt and the lame and the sick
and the blind; who told the story of the world before
history began; who traced in the minds of those who
came to ask him, other lives on earth and the promise
of more lives to be; who spoke of the Old Testament
and the New Testament as truth; who made heaven and
salvation a reward for the strong, not a dull fortress in
an inconceivable land manned by the whimpering and
the cowardly who had prayed and given alms and fled
from battle.

So in that spring I went with Hugh Lynn to Virginia
Beach, Virginia, to see his father. I expected a dark-
haired, sharp-eyed, stalwart man who walked with
gods and spoke in the language of metaphysics. I met
a mild, amiable, soft-spoken man who on the first day
changed his cigarette brand to suit mine, who allowed
me to teach him the intricacies of rummy, and who
asked me to go fishing with him. He took me into town

and bought me a soda, introduced me to the village barber, and played three sets of tennis with me. I went to bed in his house that night with complete peace. Such a nice man, I knew, would not let the devil get me.

All that, too, seems a long time ago. After that, he was my friend. I became so conversant with his life and with his work that I began to consider the idea of writing it all down. Perhaps I should have done it long ago, before I was so lost in the trees that I could not see the forest. Perhaps I should not ever have attempted it. Yet there is, in my files, an envelope labeled, "Readings," and there is, in my mind and in my heart, a certain peace.

These things are due to Edgar Cayce. Since that day when we played rummy and discussed cigarettes and drank soda and played tennis, not one of the questions which arise in the dark hours to plague the minds and hearts of men has troubled me. The soundness of my body, the temper of my mind, the quiet of my soul, are due to him. He told me who I am, and what I ought to be, and who I was in the years that are history and legend.

He informed me of the reasons for my ills and my frettings, and gave me ointments to heal. He calmed me when I was unruly, and praised me when I was meek. He set my feet again and again on the highway of humility, and held over and over again that mirror before my face in which is reflected the charge of my existence.

These things he did when asleep. Waking, he has given me roof and sustenance, friendship, and company. We have walked together through the canyons of Manhattan and over the sands of Virginia Beach. We have whiled away the hours on golf courses, and on the shaded porches of his home. He listened to my troubles, and unburdened himself to me. There is not any man for

whom I held greater love. He was, in brief, my friend.
I believed in him; I believed in his labors; I believed in
his gifts.

Therefore, the task to write his story came to me. I had
hoped that someone more worthy would be appointed. I
knew that I was inadequate, that never in my life would
a more difficult problem be set before me. It deserved
better hands. Yet the time came for its fulfillment, and
no other workman was at hand. I took it on gladly; it
was my honor.

To those who knew Edgar Cayce and his work I have
this to say: the breadth of the assignment did not escape
me. I know that on any one of the innumerable subjects
that have coursed through his thousands of readings
a book could be written. These books, in time, will be
written. My job was to break the ground, to lay down
with as much completeness and exactitude as is possible
the fundamentals of Edgar Cayce, his life, and his work.
Much had to be excluded. Things that were momentus in
their days of happening seem, in perspective, shadowy
details that stray into dull byways.

To those who come upon Edgar Cayce for the first
time, let this be a warning: it is no tale to take in stride.
Whatever else it gives you, it will give you pause. There
is not in the chapters regarding his life any program
of ballyhoo, any attempt to sell a product. His is a
document for the purpose of record. Those who would
quibble, who would point the finger of their intelligence
in scorn, who would call questions and cry for proof,
had best leave off and take again to their schoolbooks.
Here is a river for those who wish to bathe; but those
who enter it had best know how to swim.

Those who asked for his help received it. We don't
know why, but it worked. The records of thousands of
cases say the same thing. It worked for Edgar Cayce

when he was a schoolboy in Kentucky, needing help with his lessons. It worked for his friends and his loved ones, before he felt compelled to offer it to any who might ask. It has worked for thousands of sick and crippled and hopeless persons, in all states of mind and body, in all parts of the world. The hopeless have become hopeful, the suicidal have determined to live, those curious for knowledge have been satisfied, those eager for faith have found peace, and those looking for enlightenment have become wise. It may work for you.

The central problem of a biographer is to find the meaning of his subject—without a meaning, the subject is not worth writing about. The meaning of Edgar Cayce and his work, at first glance, was so obvious, it proved elusive. As I pursued it, it went higher and higher into regions of plan and law, and deeper into the tangled tragedy of man.

To most of the thousands who met him and used his powers, Edgar Cayce was an odd sort of fellow— a man with a peculiar talent: a swami in homespun, a Kentucky version of the Oracle of Delphi. Most of them liked him; many of them were grateful for the help they received; but for the most part he was treated like the doctor who cures a bad cold—nice fellow, and they'd call him again when they needed him.

Yet more than thirty years ago, in the earliest days of readings, a question was answered by a statement, which should have meant something deep and significant to all those who knew Edgar Cayce and all who thereafter met him and heard his story. The question was, "Where does this information come from?" The answer was, Edgar Cayce's mind was amenable to suggestion, the same as all subconscious minds but, in addition, it had the power to access the minds of other individuals. The subconscious mind forgets nothing. The subconscious mind of Edgar Cayce was able to communicate with other subconscious minds, both of individuals in the earth as well as those who had passed on. The implications of this are obvious: the singleness of all mind as a force, the immortality of the soul, the identification of the subconscious as the mind of the soul, and the continued development of the soul after death.

Apparently, none of these implications was drawn at the time. The statement was included in a report read before the Clinical Research Society of Boston, and was published in newspapers throughout the country. The report included physical cases in which the subconscious mind of Edgar Cayce had given diagnoses that were admittedly correct, and suggested treatments which were helpful.

If the diagnoses were correct, and the treatments were helpful, was not the statements as to the source of the information also valid?

And so, every person who thereafter met Edgar Cayce and heard his story was faced with proof — of the modern, scientific type — that the soul was immortal and one's thoughts imperishable.

Nothing whatever was made of this fact.

Fourteen years later, in Dayton, Ohio, the implications of the statement were taken up in a series of readings which gave the geography, plan, strategy and tactics of Creation, and this history of man's concern in it and in the earth.

In the intervening years, hundreds of readings were given for sick people. The diagnoses were apparently correct; the treatments, when followed, brought relief and help. The same source told the story of Creation and the history of humankind. Was the story not also correct? And if correct, was it not a rare opportunity for every person who thereafter met Mr. Cayce to know the story and to put its truth into action in his own life? Our duty is to make the truth we know and to build it into our consciousness, so that we are never unaware of it: and within our minds to shape and whet it, until it is a shining instrument that makes our every thought and action a movement toward the camps of heaven — cutting through the burned wreckage of our mistakes and build upon them a new age — not of desire, not of reason, not of science — but of spirit and faith.

Today, hate, prejudice, ignorance, misunderstanding, fear, violence, stalk the land, the sea, and the air. They will be followed by other things: hunger, pestilence, despair. This is not the cry of a Cassandra; this is not a reading of handwriting on the wall. You know this; you have heard it before. You can fill in the horrid details for yourselves.

The point is, we can no longer avoid doing something about it. Those who know this truth must live it: for them it is that thing which is more sacred and worthwhile than career, home, lands, happiness. It is what makes for them their duty.

It is what Edgar Cayce meant to you. It is what you meant to him: for why else, through forty years, should he have kept inviolate the well from which you have drawn waters to quench the thirst of your mind and heal the wounds of your body; why else, through the ages, has this been kept for you? So that you might do something about it, for yourselves and others.

Edgar Cayce did his part; he kept it for you and for me and gave it to us whenever we asked: to some of us he gave for a long time. This Association was founded on the work of Edgar Cayce.

What must you do? Let me quote from a reading, which answered this question.

Not in mighty deeds of valor, not in exultation of thy knowledge or power; but in the gentleness of the things of the spirit: love, kindness, longsuffering, patience; these thy elder brother, the Christ, has shown thee— that thou, applying them in thy associations with thy fellow man day by day, here a little, there a little, may become one with Him as He has destined that thou shouldst be! Wilt thou separate thyself? For there is nothing in earth, in heaven, in hell, that may separate thee from the love of thy God, of thy brother, save thy self.

Then, be up and doing; knowing that as thou hast met in Him those things that would exalt thy personal self . . . these ye must lose in gentleness, in patience . . . Hold fast to that faith exemplified in thy meditation, in thy counsels, in thy giving out to they fellow man. For he that hides himself in the service of his fellow man through gifts, through the promises as are in Him, hides many of the faults that have made him afraid through his experience in the earth. For it is not what one counts as knowledge that is important, nor what one would attain in material realms, but what one does about that which is known as constructive forces and influences in the experience of thy self and thy fellow man. For, as He has given, "As ye do it unto others, ye do it unto me."

Let this, then, be our promise. That in the days and years which are now to assail us, when that which would destroy our hope, our faith, our honor, is broad —we will take this truth we know and go with it to the temple of our spirit, and wait there, at the door . . . Then, when we go forth to meet that which will come against us, we shall not walk alone.

Edgar Cayce passed from this life on January 3,

1945, at 7:15 p.m. in the evening, at his home on Arctic Crescent, Virginia Beach, Virginia. Funeral services were conducted at the residence on Friday morning, January 5 by the Rev. Joseph B. Clower, former pastor of the local Presbyterian Church, and in his native town of Hopkinsville, Kentucky, on Monday morning, January 8, by the Rev. Monroe G. Schuster, pastor of the First Christian Church.

He had been ill since August 1944, when the strain of overwork pressed him down to a sick bed. For more than a year, he had worked under unbelievable handicaps. His son, the manager of the Association for Research and Enlightenment, Hugh Lynn Cayce, entered the Armed Services. At the same time, an unprecedented number of requests for readings came to Virginia Beach. Often there were more than 500 letters in the daily mail. The library, which had seemed so large when first built, was jammed with stenographers working at correspondence. Mr. Cayce himself examined every letter, and worked late into the night dictating answers.

During the morning and afternoon periods he gave not two but from eight to twelve readings. Still he could fulfill but a small portion of the applications. The others, with their tales of misfortune and suffering, weighed heavily on him. For the first time in his long life of service, he could not help everyone who asked for aid. He worked harder and harder, but the appointments ran on and on, until they were more than a year ahead of him.

His own diagnosis, given in a reading that September was that he had reached a point of complete nervous exhaustion. From this, he did not recover.

The shock of his passing is so deep that even the

most glib tongues are stilled. Once a person came to know Edgar Cayce, he thereafter could not imagine a world without him, without his readings, without his personality, his friendliness, his simple and complete Christianity. The roll of those he served is long. How many he reached through his readings, through his sixty years of Bible teaching, is incalculable. His only ambition was that after his death even more people be reached and given whatever in the readings was good and helpful.

That is the first reaction to his death — that faith must be kept with him, and his work continued. It is symbolic that his own passing was brought about largely by the change in his work; that is, he could no longer give all the readings which were requested of him, and the necessity for giving to people the information of general use in the readings was growing each day.

Everyone who knew Mr. Cayce was amazed by his strange power, but those who were privileged to know the man personally, and to observe the family life which surrounded him, came eventually to be as equally impressed by the phenomenon of a home which seemed to achieve the ideal which every person cherishes for this sacred institution. There is no doubt that the Cayce family life was unique and inspiring. Not only was there complete harmony between the four members of the family — Gertrude, Edgar, and their two sons, Hugh Lynn and Edgar Evans — but they had a genius for absorbing friends and visitors into the group in such a way that a stranger felt at home almost instantly. Many families are closely knit, but usually in such cases, the members present a united front against outsiders. The opposite was true of the Cayces. A friend of any one of them was friend of all four. Their home was always big enough for one more friend, one more visitor.

Probably this is explained by the fact that individually and collectively they tried to live Christianity. They never gave lip service to an ideal; they carried it out in deed. But the guiding genius of this organized friendliness was Mrs. Cayce. She loved her home above all things, but she conceived it to be a place of rest and comfort and refuge for not only her family, but for anyone who needed these precious blessings.

Now that he is gone, this will become the whole of the work, and as it proceeds, the real stature of Edgar Cayce will be revealed. Truly, he fulfilled the Christian ideal; he laid down his life for his friends. He was a great man. We shall not see his like again.

## What is Edgar Cayce's A.R.E.?

The Association for Research and Enlightenment, Inc. (A.R.E.) is a not-for-profit organization founded in 1931 by Edgar Cayce to research and explore transpersonal subjects such as holistic health, philosophy, dreams and dream interpretation, intuition, and personal spirituality.

Although headquartered in Virginia Beach, Virginia, the A.R.E. is a global network of individuals who offer activities and educational programs. In addition to study groups and local activities, the A.R.E. offers membership benefits and services, publications, international tours, a volunteer network, and A.R.E. contacts around the world. A.R.E. also maintains an affiliation with Atlantic University, and a massage a school, both offering a range of educational opportunities.

For additional information about programs and activities, please visit: EdgarCayce.org; or contact: A.R.E., 215 67th Street, Virginia Beach, VA 2451-2061; or call: (800) 333-4499.

Made in the USA
Middletown, DE
18 October 2024